JOSH ALAN FRIEDMAN

WHEN SEX WAS DIRTY

Miss Nude Universe
Kellie Everts
44-24-35
The preacher who dances to
help save men's souls.

CLUB HUBBA HUBBA

25 N. Hotel Street

Feral House

Designed by Sean Tejaratchi

Feral House
PO Box 39910
Los Angeles, CA 90039
Send S.A.S.E. for free catalogue of publications

info@feralhouse.com
www.feralhouse.com

10 9 8 7 6 5 4 3 2 1

Chapters of this book first appeared differently in the following publications: Hustler, Blab!, Dallas Observer, Puritan, Screw, Gallery, Spunkculture.com and Swank. "The Strikeout King," "The Rise and Fall of Al Goldstein" and "The Human Being of 42nd Street" appear here for the first time.

Names have been changed to protect the guilty in the following chapters: "God's Gift To Women," "The Strikeout King," "Winedale Nation," "Write & Fight," "The Man Who Loved Slut Dancing" and the detective in "The Rise and Fall of Al Goldstein."

The author and publishers are grateful for permission to quote extracts from lyrics: "The Oldest Profession" and "Don't Take Much" (Cy Coleman/Ira Gasman) reproduced by permission of Notable Music Co., Inc./©1997 Sony Music Entertainment, Inc.

Special Thanks: Peggy Bennett, Chloe, Richard Jaccoma, Jeff Krulik, Robert Wilonsky, Allan MacDonell, John Bowers, Monte Beauchamp, Jeff Goodman, Adam Parfrey, Kevin Page and Earl Browning III.

CONTENTS

WHEN SEX WAS DIRTY

...IN NEW YORK

...IN TEXAS

...IN NEW YORK

CHAPTER ONE

GOD'S GIFT TO WOMEN

I had just suffered a month hanging out with New York's reigning "strikeout king"—an otherwise cunning men's magazine editor named Sammy Grubman. Poor Grubman spent his summer dreaming up endless ruses to score women—bogus rock video auditions, swimsuit contests, photo "test shoots" for his mag. Dumbstruck, I joined him in his nightly rounds at the Palladium and Studio 54 as he hit upon ballrooms of females. In his rumpled suit, skinny black tie, thick glasses, with nasal whine and Sen-Sen breath, I watched him viciously strike out under the rotating disco ball. I even got into the rhythm of failure with him, tossing out some dumb pickup lines myself. Losing wind after a hundred No's, he repositioned to the girls' powder room. The most common retort from spandexed chicks exiting, as Grubman propositioned each for a drink, was simply, "Fuck you." By 4 a.m., reeling from the dread of such monumental rejection, Grubman would bomb himself to sleep with codeine pills.

I too began wondering whether all women in New York were paranoid men-haters, terrified to smile at a stranger. Or was it just Grubman, rubbing off on me?

During this time, a fringe show-biz agent pal of ours named Shark began relating tales of the greatest barroom pickup artist alive. Shark reflected upon his own glory years in the 1960s. His organs malfunctioning from middle-aged alcoholism, Shark grew moist in reminiscence over the only activity that really mattered—sliding his pecker into trainloads of girls. He called this perpetual state of scoring a "roll."

"It's a beautiful thing, being on a *roll*," Shark recalled, his voice hoarse from substance abuse. "Catching the rhythm and keeping it up night after night. While you're fucking one broad, you're planning tomorrow's menu. You establish your turf, your nightclubs, your clique of celebs, then the broads flock to *you* each night. But once you're out of the rhythm, Jack, it's *very* hard to get back in."

Shark definitely seemed to have lost his chops as a pick-up artist, along with his best clients and his dough. He ran a skid-row agency, Tops Models, for mostly unemployable bush-leaguers—A&P checkout girls and bar hostesses with big dreams and bigger tits. Real lookers some were, but cursed by being an inch too short for Ford, a pound too heavy for Elite. They were unschooled and gawky in their runway gait. Some had white-trash bruises that healed slowly.

But Shark had become spiritually rejuvenated by the discovery of this protégé. He referred to him as the Stud. Through the Stud, he could vicariously live out the longest roll of his career.

"The kid's incredible, like DiMaggio on a hitting streak," claimed the agent. "There's no one can touch him. He's got 15 broads a day callin', beggin' to go out, 10 more from last week beggin' for seconds. Walks out of clubs with three, four at a time, the best-lookin' ones. He's not interested in amenities, he don't send flowers. He don't wanna know their names, their jobs, where they're from... I hung out with Namath. I hung out with Elvis. I hung out with Engelbert. None of these guys could hold the Stud's jockstrap."

I was suddenly struck by the antithesis of Grubman. The Stud seemed heroic, swimming upstream like an erect salmon against the tide of '80s abstinence in the face of AIDS. The Stud's reputation drove Grubman crazy. I decided to do two articles: One on New York's premier pickup artist, and then one on New York's foremost strikeout king (a title no man would relish). I would take a journey like Gulliver; I had been to the land of the Lilliputians. Now I would visit the land of giants.

GOD'S GIFT

Mike Florio is the Stud's name, a special effects man in Local 52 of the movie business. At 31, he's been on a 12-year roll, according to Shark, who passed the Stud my number. On the phone Florio is a far cry from Cary Grant. The timbre and accent of his voice could be that of any Brooklyn garage mechanic. Florio makes it clear, at first, that he hates men. "I always go out alone," he explains. "I don't need dead weight dragging along."

A nephew of rib restaurateur Tony Roma, Florio began his career as a stunt man on *Kramer Vs. Kramer*. The production chief wanted him fired, Florio recalls, for "bangin' dozens of chicks on the set." So this very morning, a decade later, he reports for work on the Michael Douglas film, *Fatal Attraction*. He's setting up special rain effects, which he feels will garner him an Oscar nomination. The same production chief is on the movie, says he's impressed with how Mike's "matured," become professional, not chasing skirts on the job. "Then SAG calls the set this morning," huffs Mike, "claims there are four sex harassment complaints about me, looking up girls' dresses and stuff."

The Stud claims to be immune from disease, refuses to wear protection: "The last time I wore a rubber it ended up in 40 pieces." As we talk by phone, the Stud's call-waiting device is constantly clicking. These are the frustrated attempts of girls phoning around the clock. Mike clicks in some of his call-waiting gals, then phones a list of this week's conquests, with me listening on the party line. His voice is a haunting reminder of a night in which they slept with a stranger. In a dozen calls, the Stud arranges dates with roommates of girls who aren't home; a secretary will risk being fired and see him that instant; a girl in bed with a fever will come out that night; three girls are each assigned to visit a different club—Arena, Limelight and the Milk Bar—pick up another girl, then come to his apartment, at two-hour intervals. Each girl whispered her willingness to sleep with him again. Mike has fucked many of them up the ass, he says, within an hour of meeting each one.

Perhaps these were self-destructive wackos, from amongst the exploding buyer's market of girls out there. Nightclubs are bursting with available females. There must be a dozen Studs in every city, I told Shark. Why glamorize the bastard in print?

"You've heard him with one type of girl over the phone," Shark insisted. "But he's a high roller. Take him out. There're a lot of supermodels at the clubs around Christmas. The Stud's as good at scoring broads as Picasso was at painting."

That Saturday, I made the rounds with one of New York's premier pickup artists. Strikeout kings, read on.

Café Pacifico, 10 p.m.

We decide to rendezvous at Pacifico, a Columbus Avenue café which looks like a rejected stage set from *A Clockwork Orange*. "You'll *know* who I am," he predicted over the phone. Sure enough, several girls are milling about the front barstool. The hottest blonde in the joint is stroking some bloke's generous brown curls. He's wearing black suede boots, pleated slacks, a T-shirt under a fluffy cockpit jacket that momentarily makes him resemble a Saint Bernard pup. It's the Stud. He looks like some indeterminable pretty-boy corporate rock star. Somebody girls can't quite pinpoint.

"I love this chick. She's so sweet." Mike narrates the situation as if she's not in the room. Having just arrived himself, he removes his coat, professing to love all his jackets. He has dozens. Each jacket carries "a unique vibe," whether it cost 20 bucks or $500. As a matter of fact, some chick wouldn't leave his apartment last night. He finally tossed her clothes in the hall to get her out. But the heap included one of his beloved jackets, a Willywear, which she kept. It was like losing a friend. The Stud had no way to contact her to retrieve the jacket. Why get bogged down with names when you're banging several chicks a night?

The blonde stroking his hair has just signed with some new modeling agency. She's dripping with homemade jewelry. Her painfully long legs are twisting around the barstool, and she's terribly bored with everything in the world except this foxy guy who just took the adjacent stool. The Stud whispers in her ear, to her utter delight. Then her girlfriend enters the restaurant.

It's the girlfriend's 24th birthday, they're out to celebrate. Round of champagne, says Mike, an $18 pouring for the three of them.

"Yeah, I like this chick," he says aloud of the blonde, "but I like her girlfriend better." And *voila*, the brunette birthday girl, an expensively decked-out lady with profound cleavage, is slayed by one insincere Mike Florio smile. The Stud reaches around the wall where the bartender unquestioningly allows him to rearrange the mood lighting for the entire bar. In this darkened atmosphere, he takes the birthday girl's hands, introduces himself as her birthday present, and begins soul kissing. The blonde model is miffed, a spurned pout on her haughty face. I feel invisible to both girls. The Stud's girl-mechanic hands travel over the outside of Birthday Girl's body like sonar, taking a reading on what's underneath those Bergdorf threads.

"Let's leave this dump and go to Columbus," demands the Stud, to both dames.

"I don't wanna go," whines the rejected blonde, swaying her jewelry to Huey Lewis on the jukebox. "I wanna dance at the Palladium."

"*I don't wanna*," sing-songs the Stud, in mock imitation. "The Palladium's a dump."

In actuality, the Palladium, Stringfellow's and Nell's have banned Mike from their premises—as pool sharks are banned from pool halls.

"You're giving me trouble," spits the blonde.

"The world is full of trouble," counters Mike. "Trouble makes the world go round. But imagine how much fun we can have when the trouble stops... ."

The blonde giggles at this lame philosophy. Florio's style is to *parody* pickup clichés, with a wink—women love to laugh along, part of a spontaneous joke. Birthday Girl has her hands all over him, and pleads with her stubborn friend to follow us guys to Columbus. But the Stud feels he's given them both too much of his time, and stands to leave. Birthday Girl is deflated. But they exchange phone numbers. She enters his right into her address book in pen. He takes hers on a napkin, which he'll blow his nose with later.

Columbus, 10:45

The way most guys work a bar, Mike explains, reminds him of a moronic stop-action silent film. They flicker around in a circle. Mike centers himself at the middle barstool, where he can track all girls coming through. He sucks them over in two's and three's. "I've got eyes in the back of my head for chicks," he says, surveying the room like a speed reader. "That table's all married; forget the blonde in the corner, she's with a Colombian coke dealer; I already fucked the shit outta that table…"

Columbus Restaurant is this year's celebrity hangout on Columbus Avenue. Its vacuous soul is that of a mall—there's no hearth, just unadorned windows for celeb gazing. The Stud comes through like a barroom Frankenstein. Ice-breaking one-liners spew out rapid-fire.

"Hey, I like you, what can I do about it?" *Bam*, one chick at his side. "A woman is a noun. I am a verb." *Zap*, a second girl takes up position. "I got brand new bed sheets, never been slept in." *Kapow*. "Take off your hat, what're you trying to cover up, chemotherapy?" he cracks, grabbing the hat off a passing girl's head.

Before you know it, he's got an admiration society. All are TKO's, any of them ready to leave with Mike should he so desire. I am virtually invisible at his side. Even the two at Pacifico were scored as TKO's. "They'll call," Mike shrugs, matter-of-factly, "I'll bang both of 'em."

Every line he speaks with blushing boyish charm, a sarcastic, Ultrabrite smile, creating instant camaraderie. "I'm married," one girl retorts to his come-on.

"That's your problem," says the Stud, quickly disinterested, his Saint Bernard puppy expression fraught with disgust, making her feel it really *is* her problem.

When Florio sees a chick he likes, all he merely has to do is "Give her one of these." He demonstrates waving his finger with effortless superiority, like Buddy Love in *The Nutty Professor*. This draws the attention of two curious girls. He introduces himself as the "lead singer of Cinderella."

"Yeah, I'm headlining The Garden next week, wanna go?" One of the chicks nervously jots his phone number down, thinking she's scored some heavy metal clod. "Yeah, gimme a call, I'll be waitin' by the phone *like a dog*."

After several Heinekens, the Stud hiccups obnoxiously into every girl's face at the Columbus meat rack. He intermittently apologizes, or snaps at them to "Shut up!"

"Wha'd he say?!" demands some guy, joining his girlfriend after a respite in the restroom. "Should I belt him?"

"… I hate men," replies the Stud, with a cosmic sigh to the complainant. He leans over in confidence toward two mouseburger girls, out of the side his mouth: "I'm so horny. Just gotta get laid. But there's no *good* pussy here tonight, you dig?" He hiccups in their faces.

"Please don't do that in our ears," say the homely girls, unflattered. The Stud gets more obnoxious with each downed beer.

"Would you prefer I do it up your ass? *Brrappp.* You know, you two remind me of Mutt & Jeff. I won't say who's Mutt."

The Stud approaches a group of hardened, out-of-work actresses in their early 30s. They're indignant over his demeanor, having overheard the last 10 minutes. They're onto his game and they don't approve.

"I'll tell you something, all you women," he announces, with histrionic presence. "If you didn't own a pussy, you wouldn't have a friend in the world." After a half-dozen beers, the Stud seems to have slipped. This group doesn't want him. So, he blows his cover and confides to them he's a barroom pickup artist: "I'm God's gift to women. I really am. That's why he put me here—for you, and you and you. I live for women. I was born for you. I have a great job, in the movies, I work two, three hard days a week. Make lots of money, then come out at night for pussy. If I don't get it here, I go across the street. If I don't get it from you, I'll get it from her. But I'll *get* it," he shrugs.

The group listens with amused disdain. "I have a great penthouse apartment, full of *life*. It's filled with plants and Pacific Ocean fish tanks." Indeed, the Stud keeps two sharks on the premises in his living room aquarium. The first is a one-and-a-half-foot leopard shark, the other a three-foot nurse shark. Both are capable of taking a serious bite out of a man, but they have a hypnotizing effect on women.

Still holding their attention, Mike quiets down to a soulful confession. "Don't analyze me in 10 minutes, baby, I got hours." Florio never had sex as a teenager, he says, was rejected throughout high school. Then when he was 19, he fell deeply in love with a girl. They planned to marry. Shortly after, one day, a doctor told him his father had 10 months to live. This hit him like a sledgehammer, since his dad was closest to him in the world. Thank heavens his girlfriend's father was chief radiologist at New York Hospital, who could provide the saving care Mike's father needed. But on the same day he planned to ask his fiancée for her family's help, she showed up arm in arm with another guy. Mike was dumped on the spot, at New York Hospital. "From then on," the Stud recalled, "I decided that *I'm* the one who'll do the fucking over, not girls."

The actresses are moved. They're talking softly with Mike now. Three more TKO's for the Stud. "I'm God's gift to women!" he bellows, a jungle cry to the bar at large.

"God's gift to women is a dildo!" screams back some drunk.

"Here, here," toast some hearty male voices at the bar.

Florio needs some grub before he can reach a second wind. The hostess seems hot for him and gives us a reserved table. This is an exclusive area at night, beyond the meat rack. The table next to us contains four young, high-toned models, strategically placed at Columbus' front window like an advertisement. Some heavy metal millionaire sits with them. At the table in front of them, however, is a big-time beauty with several male escorts. "Point me to whoever you want, I'll get her," he says, like a hunting dog. I tell him to turn around for the first true 10 of the evening. This knockout will be his target for tonight, he decides, deciphering her body as if wearing X-ray specs.

The moment the heavy metal idiot goes to the john, the Stud reaches over and taps a model on the shoulder. She's a black-haired heartbreaker with a cute, upturned nose job and pyramid tits.

"What's your name?"

"Courtney."

"Hi, Courtney. Joe Perry," says the Stud, extending a sturdy handshake. For the rest of the evening, he'll pose as a member of Aerosmith. "Say, Courtney," he goes, waving her closer in confidence. "Who's *that*?"

"Why, that's Carol Alt," says Courtney. Carol has a natural, outdoorsy look, without much makeup. She's wearing something like riding pants, as if she just stepped in from an afternoon of British polo. An elaborate fur is draped around her chair, and she's seated with three male chaperones. She's one of the world's five top models, yet she doesn't look so self-consciously *modelly* as the girls behind her.

The Stud has heard of her. "Look how *bored* she is," he ascertains, as if she were in dire need of rescue. He can tell she goes to bed by one o'clock from her clear skin. "Got to work fast."

Carol starts table-hopping. She stops by Mike Tyson's table, and he rises to kiss her cheek, looking pretty as a *GQ* cover after his three-round KO over Trevor Berbick. She schmoozes with the owners of Columbus, then Danny Aiello. Then she stops at Courtney's table. Warren Beatty takes a table, sits there innocently, not bothering anybody. "Look at him, he can't even get laid anymore," says the Stud. Neither can a member of Kiss, striking out left and right (anonymous without makeup and costume).

The Stud fidgets over the time the young models are spending with Alt. "These chicks are gonna fuck it up for me. They're all like monkeys together." Alt returns to her table, slips on the fur. All the minor models at Courtney's table put on *their* fur coats. "Like monkeys," he repeats, making his move.

Florio sits right down at Carol Alt's table, introducing himself as the lead guitarist of Aerosmith, about to leave to play with Gino Vanelli, and headline the Garden next month. He blurts out a few lines from "Walk This Way," with a high cackle. Tells her he took lessons from the guitar player in the Tonight Show Orchestra as a kid. She says she was about to call it an evening at midnight. The Stud brings her back to our table, offering his last forkful of chicken pot pie.

"No, really, I'm just having one Scotch tonight," she giggles.

"A Scotch in Carol Alt's perfect bod?" he gasps, incredulously. She's sweet, innocent and gullible. One of her chaperones is a bulky ex-Hell's Angel and Vietnam vet, keeping an eye on her. The Stud says how much he would enjoy dancing with her at the China Club. Alt agrees to go. She's very polite toward me, whom the Stud has introduced as his manager (an incarnation I shudder from).

While she goes through the saying-goodbye ceremonies to friends, the Stud's table is approached by several pairs of women who seem to know him. Some are former one-night affairs. Being invisible next to this caballero, I must suppress my ego. "Just remember," Shark the agent had cautioned, "don't even try to compete. Most guys' egos couldn't handle a night with him." The Stud lays out tonight's situation to the girls, who shrug and wish him luck. They are *rooting* for him to fuck the model.

The Stud engages two hot-looking chicks as he's about to exit. "C'mon, let's go dancing at the China Club," he orders, as though they were anything but strangers. Both accept. They're from Oklahoma, and have a BMW outside, offering us a lift there. But the Stud peers first into a double-parked Lincoln Town Car, pretending his chauffeur has disappeared.

Jackie Mason, at a nearby table, was confounded as to why so many broads came and went from our table. His lawyer, Jesse Vogel, one of Mason's entourage of alter cocker flunkies, is propositioning blondes, and asks the Oklahoma girls if they'd like to sit for a drink with a famous Jewish comedian, headlining 16 weeks on Broadway.

"I can play a romantic lead," declares Mason to his table. "Why shouldn't I? That ugly dumb bastard, Dangerfield, was the romantic lead in that last picture, what was it?"

"*Back To School*," comes the table.

"Yeah, he gets the goil, that Sally-what's-her-name, he was a romantic lead. And you mean to tell me, this skinny putz, wid the big nose and glasses, this bent-over sickeningly ugly weasel, Woody Allen, can play romantic leads, and I can't? He can sleep with Diane Keaton or Mia Farrow?"

Both girls decline Mason's lawyer's invitation, waiting patiently for the Stud.

"You think I have a chance?" Florio wonders, his first glimmer of insecurity about scoring the supermodel. Quick deliberation—should he *walk* Carol Alt's party to China, or get into these chicks' BMW? Best Carol see him exit with other girls, he decides. We hop into the Okies' car. Alt shrugs—oh, well, there goes Mr. Aerosmith.

The Stud makes the Okies park before a fire hydrant at the side of China Club. They're afraid of getting a ticket or towed. Florio guarantees he'll pay any ticket, and offers them full usage of his "limo" if they get towed, until he can bail out their car. They believe him. The Okies park.

China Club, Half-Past Midnight

The Okie girls expect to be whooshed in for free on the Stud's comet. Instead, he ditches them at the door. Florio claims to have "lost his pass" to the China Club box office marm. He flashes his Ultrabrite smile, and bullshits past the door charge.

It is a matter of honor that the Stud *never* pays the stiff entrance to clubs. Stringfellow's, for example, is the type of joint that considers it utterly uncool to admit human beings from New Jersey. The last straw occurred when Mike showed up with Miss America of 1980, her sister and an Elite model. "Just because you're with three gorgeous girls, you think you can come in for free?" sneered manager John Hawkins, with a British laugh. "That'll be a hundred bucks." The Stud started a fracas, threatened to hit the guy. The cops hustled Florio into a squad car, telling him he was going to the Pig Bar, a nearby establishment.

"But I don't want to go to the Pig Bar," Florio protested.

"You either come with us to the Pig Bar or get arrested." Florio accepted a police escort to the Pig Bar.

Now at the crowded China Club, Florio has bigger fish to fry. Alt's entourage won't arrive for 15 minutes. He has time to exercise his pick-up muscles, do some warm-ups. The Stud grabs a reserved table in a cordoned-off side area. Already, girls are flocking around, something I take for granted, the world is always like this.

A tall blonde hugs him, saying, "Hey, how're ya?" Mike leans to me, whispering, "Never saw her in my life." Girls often approach, acting like they know him. This one's an ex-Playboy Club bunny from the recently defunct New York branch. He plays it as if he remembers her, says she's even gained weight. Her girlfriend eagerly takes a seat on the Stud's right. A third female sits at the table, vying for Mike's attention. She also claims to know him. Reminds him that he fucked her six months ago, a memorable night. "Sorry," he shrugs, "I guess it wasn't so memorable to me."

The Stud's act is so well oiled, he can slip and slide women through these seats like a Detroit assembly line. As the big blonde is vacating her chair, the Stud simultaneously reaches over to an adjacent table, clutching the hand of a brunette stranger conversing with some fellow. She takes his hand, continuing her talk. Neither have even made eye contact. But then she sort of slithers into the vacant seat within seconds of the blonde's departure. An average-looking girl, overwhelmed by this groovy guy grabbing her hand. But she didn't even see the sucker, she must have responded to some primal musk.

"What's your name?" she asks.

"Does it matter?" The Stud isn't interested in names, occupations, he could care less about sentimental dolls girls keep by their pillows, or cooking tips. I remember Shark's initial testimony—"He don't send flowers, he don't care where they're from. He just lives to fuck."

"What do you do?" asks the enchanted girl.

"Does it matter? I thought you recognized me... Do you wanna fuck me?"

The girl's face closes in until they lock tongues, mouth to mouth. She's a goner, you can see stars around her head.

"Your place or mine?" he whispers. She practically comes in her seat, needing a spatula to be removed. She then gathers her composure and explains she visits the China Club often. If she's seen walking out with him, it will be assumed she's going to sleep with him. If the door bouncers see this more than once, they'll think she's a "slut." Therefore, they should exit separately and meet by the corner payphone. As she runs her hands through his hair, the Stud's head spins to some foxy chick in the aisle, and he excuses himself for a minute.

"You seem to have landed my friend," I suggest.

"I know," she smiles, primping in her pocketbook mirror. "But *who* is he?"

"All I can tell you is a lot of girls have been after him tonight. But I haven't seen him take to any like you."

"I know," she glows, confident of her big score.

I ask if she'll go to his place or hers, and she says definitely his. I ask her what she sees in him, having known him a total of five minutes.

"I love long hair," she says. "I want to run my hands through his hair all night. You know, I didn't really feel sexy tonight. But he brought it out in me. He's very oral, and so am I," she squeals, eyes widening in anticipation, as though I'm not even there.

"Are you ready?" she asks the Stud, upon his return.

The Stud is intently staring off in the distance, whale-watching for Carol Alt. She repeats herself. He gazes beyond, giving her the silent treatment. She looks at her watch, lights a cig, a bit confused, not yet hip to the game. The Stud turns to me and blurts, "I ain't gonna fuck *that*," hitching his thumb toward her. She tugs his sleeve. He swats her hand like a fly.

"Hey, what's going on?" she demands, horrified.

"I don't wanna fuck *you* any more," he says, sour-faced, like he's dealing with total shit. She doesn't believe her ears. "I don't wanna fuck you any more," he repeats. "Get lost."

"What!?" After it sinks in, she puts her hands on her hips. "Kind of brutal, huh?"

But Mike's not even paying attention, spotting his big-time prey at the entrance. The reject is mumbling incoherently, can't quite bring herself to accept the humiliation.

"Look—" says the Stud, with sympathetic compromise. "You still wanna fuck me, you have to go pick up another girl to come along. One better-looking than yourself."

She's shell-shocked, but starts to consider. "Jailhouse Rock" comes over the house speakers, and the Stud lets out a battle cry of "Everybody wants to suck my cock!" in sync with the chorus. He's off in the crowd, lots of familiar faces from Columbus, like part of a duck-breeding migration. "Ya gonna sit in on drums with my band at the Garden?" he asks Mason Reese, passing the orange dwarf whilst following Alt to a prime table.

He's pure gentleman now, won't use any low blows in acquiring the supermodel. The Stud is past his feeding time—by now, he could have been home and back for seconds. Alt is clearly in charge of her entourage, it's her table. The Stud and I are invited to take seats.

"Are we mixing in London or L.A.?" The Stud asks me.

"Whichever city will let you in," I say, cringing at the thought of it. Sometimes Mike forgets which rock star he's already impersonated, and blows his cover with the prey. But this more likely happens at home, by which time he can convince the girl she should be flattered he went through the trouble.

The Stud guides the supermodel onto the China Club dance floor, where they appear like royalty. They get along famously, doubled up with laughter after four dances. She even requests "Walk This Way" from the DJ. But then the million-dollar model reveals she is happily married to hockey star Ron Greschner of the New York Rangers. The Stud trudges back to our table. "Something's wrong with the way she feels," he confides. "She doesn't have as great a body as I thought. If she was available, I would have had her already... There's not a woman on this earth I can't pick up when I'm hot as a pistol."

The Stud professes a code of honor that respects newlyweds or women in love with other men (unless they so much as wink first). And so, the Stud disappears into the horizon to divide and conquer new female territory. He leaves me with the supermodel.

She's out celebrating her father's birthday tonight, though she vowed to be home by one o'clock. He was a decorated fireman who passed away several years ago. I ask her a stupid question, like how many endangered species went into her fur. "It keeps me warm," she sighs, curling an eyebrow with interest. "So, you believe in things?"

God's Gift To Women reappears 10 minutes later to take his last shot. He tugs on Alt's elbow like a child trying to get a grownup's attention. But she doesn't respond. Nevertheless, he's lined up a pair of sisters, two barroom Doublemint twins in their early 20s. Both are running their hands over his leather cockpit jacket, caressing his neck, purring and anxious to get back to his big brass bed. They look like two dumb little lambs being led off to slaughter. He'll give them the thrill of a year, then show them to the door after he comes. Maybe he'll hit the Milk Bar before 4 a.m. for another score. Valuable minutes are ticking away, and he has to make his quota. Carol, meanwhile, has rejected him. But she engages me in an awfully friendly conversation, and it's the first time tonight I don't feel invisible.

Postscript

Several months after my rounds with the Stud, I spotted a most unusual patron slumped down in his seat in the dank third-floor Triple Treat Theatre at Show World. It was the Stud! He slumped further in his seat, leather cockpit jacket unfurled around his neck, hoping I didn't see him. Like a dejected puppy dog, he finally owned up that it was indeed himself and shook my hand. In the company of dreaded men—legions of unlaid masturbators, to boot—he looked around, sizing up the place. Some porn starlet was onstage. "You come here?" he asked. I was making my weekly rounds for *Screw*'s Naked City listings, my weekly column.

"Hey, this is my first time here," he swore. "My first time ever." And then he let out a trademark sarcastic chuckle and choked a bit, like the cat who ate the canary.

CHAPTER TWO

THE STRIKEOUT KING

The I.D. Girls

A s any network news program told you with relish, drinking by teenage girls was on the rise. Lushes by 18. So many a teen alcoholic got caught in a bind when New York State raised its legal drinking age to 21 in 1985. Nymphs who'd been swigging it down legally suddenly had to come into the city for fake I.D.'s. Enter the Playlands of Times Square.

A pal of mine, Sammy Grubman, took immediate notice of this political situation. A men's magazine editor in his thirties, Sammy spent many a lunch hour enraptured by the teenagers lining up at Playland headquarters— Broadway between 42nd & 43rd Streets. Mobs of boppers would subway into Times Square at school break to purchase fake I.D.'s. The I.D. girls became a New York phenomenon.

Sammy had a self-admitted weakness for young bloods, and he gazed for hours at girls in braces. His office was just around the corner, and since the liquor age rose, he often returned late from lunch, drooling like a dingo. They subwayed in from Jersey, Queens, Brooklyn, the Bronx and Staten Isle. Sammy imagined them later in evening: "Carloads of liquored-up dirty girls going 100 mph, talking about blowjobs until they get into a wreck."

The Playland off 42nd & Broadway became the most booming fake I.D. franchise in the city. (This was the same location where I got my *Screw* press pass laminated every year.) Gals filled out a form at the counter, in English or Spanish, which was then promptly punched out along with a tiny Polaroid onto an official-looking $8 card. *Voila*, they instantly came of age. A bartender's signal to pour. The girls left squealing, their freshly laminated Times Square I.D.'s at the ready, so they could go out club-hopping with their underage boyfriends and become drunk-driving fatalities.

"Let's go to a bar and get fucked up!" said a Puerto Rican tamale to her accomplice as they nervously scattered out of Playland one Friday. A new wave entered, affecting phony tough-girl facades. "Remember, you gotta be anonymous," said the ringleader to her girlfriends. Some lost their nerve at the entrance. Strangers to this funky Times Square locale—the Crossroads of the Third World—they were afraid they'd be stopped, questioned or arrested.

"You've got bumper crops of 'em coming in to Penn Station from Long Island," said Sammy, leering near the arcade entrance. "They have braver girlfriends who've done it first, told 'em how ya walk eight blocks up from Penn Station. This is the first time they've been to the city, they don't know anything about it, they're terrified of getting lost. They're doing something naughty, they think they're going out drinking in the city. After they buy the I.D., they look around a few blocks on the way back to Penn, but they won't find anything. Maybe they'll stop in McDonald's, the only thing they recognize. Then they run back to the train before dark. That's the whole I.D. Girl itinerary... Here's a new I.D. train from Great Neck," Sammy sputtered. "Look at King Bozo, the protector," he fizzled, over their young male chaperone.

"You can't overestimate their intelligence," explained Sammy, who rarely ever actually talked to one. "They'd be terrified if some older guy came on. There's no way to pick them up. They don't know the Palladium or Studio 54, you can't show them tickets, they've never heard of anything. You'd have to tell them something they can relate to in TV terms, like you're an actor trying to make it in New York, something they've seen on soaps. You're a photographer, you shoot rock bands like Kiss.

"Look, there's a group that just went shopping, they're dressed just like a commercial for The Gap." The girls giddily made themselves up in a photo booth mirror before their Polaroids were snapped. They wore leg-warmers and pre-faded jeans. "You also get your real *goyisha* Dirty Girls," he added, panting after a new group entered, dressed up to get messed up. "You might as well just pass out," sighed Sammy at his pervert's perch.

Just what makes them so appealing?

"Young sluts are adventurous," Sammy explained. "They don't smell, everything that comes out of them is sweet. Another few years, they start to stink."

Trains indeed pulled into Penn Station with new waves of I.D. Girls, images Sammy would toss and turn over. But he never had the gumption to approach them. He knew well the dangers of procuring jailbait, what with cops and plainclothes all over this corner.

"There goes Mr. Racial Ambiguity," he said of another chaperone, wishing it could be him.

The Palladium

I accompanied Sammy on his nightly rounds pursuing females by the thousand. He always returned home alone. An industrious fellow, Sammy's work-a-day-world was permeated with endless ruses: "All my desires, the magazines, my movie company dealings, the exercise tapes, all stem from wanting to meet girls," said Sammy. "Every idea I have, every motivation, comes from my obsession with girls. I hate the Palladium, you'd never get me there unless I had a good friend giving a party or some business deal. It's repulsive, the music is sickening, the people are pathetic. It's only good for taking some dumb slut, using my invites to proposition some bimbo who has to wait on line and can't get in, but thinks it's hot shit to go. If I had a girlfriend, I'd never go there. My idea of a great evening is to go to Chinatown, order off-the-menu, run home, fuck her, then watch TV in bed while she tells me how great I am, how happy she is to be with me."

In his unkempt midtown apartment, littered with watches and hot Panasonic racing bike parts (not his), Sammy splashed on a handful of Paco Raban cologne, arranged his skinny black tie and donnned the rumpled black Brooks Brothers suit bought wholesale at Syms. He'd worn it all week. His black glasses were thick, as was the scent of sen-sen upon his breath. He popped two Valium. He carried a pocket full of special passes to upcoming oh-so-exclusive Palladium events, which he would flash to females. These were easily obtained by New York media mockeys like Sammy—whose primary vocation was nine-to-five editor of *Oui* magazine. We cabbed it to the Palladium.

Sammy also fronted a semi-legitimate office for exercise and swimsuit models seeking "print work." He called such prospective amateurs "Cargo Models."

"Fly 'em up for a look, if I'm not satisfied, send 'em back down in five minutes, it's only a few hours to Miami. Are you kidding, a modeling interview in New York, fashion capital of the world? They gab to all their friends, ba-bah-bah-bah, I'm flying to New York. This is the dream they see in every stupid TV show and magazine. But ya gotta ask to see *all* their pictures, not just skin photos. You wanna see their contact sheets, any stupid Polaroids. You can never tell from model pictures, they always look different, you tell 'em to Fed Ex all of 'em up quick. That way you can almost insure it won't be a total bust. Some models look terrible in person, they're great picture girls, not fuck girls. You need a front, an office with the bullshit, a secretary, sit there in a suit with phones ringing, a switchboard. A front is essential. Have 'em sign some stupid paper, makes it look important."

Two of his recent prospects were the Bai Sisters (pronounced *bah-hi*). Sometimes, he hired girls for an actual project, and in this case, he flew the Bai Sisters up for a video box cover. He arranged the shoot to take place at the Palladium. "It was terrible, a disaster session," Sammy moans. "The Bai Sisters have huge tits, like half watermelons. But I noticed they sagged a bit. They wore these huge wire bras that threw me off. Wouldn't let me touch 'em. Then the cameraman, the Palladium guy, the lighting guy, all went crazy as soon as the tits came out, started using every come-on they could think of. I demanded that they behave professionally, but they didn't and I couldn't control 'em. The sisters freaked out."

Sammy cut their visit short and sent the sisters back to Miami. He waved them off at the airport with a fond "Bah-hi!"

Outside the Palladium—AKA "the torture club"— were what Sammy called the "Line-Up Girls." 50 of them, a bit older than the afternoon I.D. Girls, anxiously awaited selection for the honor of paying tonight's $10 entrance. Exclusion was the currency here. *Let's all get excited about parties to which we're uninvited.* Even more rarefied were Friday nights in the Mike Todd Room, where Ladies Only roamed. The backroom bar was known as Shescape. Not even Don Johnson and David Lee Roth were allowed to crash it.

Hundreds of chumps also braved the line each night, raising their hands like schoolboys, dying to get in. A few gutter Blacks outside worked a tired scam ("I'm friends with the do' man, gimme twenty, I getcha in.") Sammy scanned the line. One chick, with boyfriend, struck up a friendly chat. When she asked how he acquired the special passes he flaunted, Sammy said, "We're bigshots from Hollywood." Sammy cemented a friendship with the Palladium's mailroom clerk for invitations. Feeling gregarious, he handed an extra pass to her. he conceded to me, "half your power is lost" at this point.

Sammy presented two passes to the goons at the door. Once inside, he set sight on his first prey at the bar. He took a seat next to the lass, but couldn't rev his engine for a few minutes. Finally, he hit with the lamest of come-ons: "What do you do for a living?"

She rolled her eyes and soured her expression without an answer. Three of her girlfriends strolled over, all oblivious to Sammy and myself. They were bubbling over about Boy George, who was in the Mike Todd Room upstairs. The four were trading off their one special pass to get in. Sammy volunteered that he possessed a pass and that "Boy George works" for his company.

"Would you like to meet Boy George?"

The sour-faced cutie became animated, suddenly interested as Sammy pulled out abundant Mike Todd Room passes. "Would you like me to introduce you?"

"Would you?!" she cried.

"No," said Sammy. "You could have said 'No Thanks,' or said you weren't interested politely. But you made a face and didn't answer. You sit there for 20 minutes in the Palladium then get upset when some guy approaches? Fuck you. Now I'm leaving to go up and see Boy George."

Sammy walked off smugly, having scored himself a rare TKO.

"They're just girls, sometimes out of high school," said Sammy, veering off to observe the female powder room exit. "Yet trying to land one requires all the cunning of a corporate takeover."

We walked upstairs where the cocktail party was in progress for Boy George. Boy and 500 of his very closest friends. There was an open bar manned by a butch bartender. "I like seeing barmaids in uniforms, with their hats tilted at a jaunty, subservient angle," said Sammy, from the side of his mouth. The butch bartender happened to be a charter member of Women Against Pornography, I would later learn. She spotted Sammy. As Grubman recovered our drinks to leave, a large bouncer laid a beefy hand on Sammy's shoulder. He ordered him to halt.

"I thought it was Open Bar?" cried Sammy.

"*You* pay," yelled the bartendress from behind the bar, eyeing him with venom.

The Mike Todd room had a more elite clientele, barring most Line-Up Girls. Remember, *exclusion* was what made the Palladium's engine tick. While models flitted about us, Sammy imparted this theory: "Their whole career is trading their body one way or another to get ahead. What's modeling but a life of what they think is glamour, meeting famous people, traveling, show biz? So they're another form of hooker, basically.

"Unfortunately, a beautiful girl is the highest status symbol in the world. I don't care what car you have, what clothes, how much money. When you walk in the room with a beautiful girl, even if you look like a slob in jeans, everyone thinks you must be hot shit, you must know something... 'Look at that old fuck with the models, he must be the owner of a famous design company.'"

A Continental chap named Fritz was Special Events coordinator at the Palladium. Sammy didn't fancy Euro Trash. Every one of the regulars here who seemed to score with models was named Lars, Horst, Otto, Helmut, Hans, Sven, Rudolph or David. A Venezuelan beauty queen, whose airfare to New York was paid for by one of Sammy's ventures, escaped his clutches. Instead, she made her way through every Tom, Dick and Adolf here at the Mike Todd Room. Fritz, a high-roller with the broads, let out a cosmic sigh of cigarette smoke.

"I'm so sick of zeze hard, stressed-out professional chicks with zere insane schedules," he told Sammy.

"How'd you do with the Venezuelan?" asked Sammy.

"Ze girl takes so much coke—not just enough to get high, enough to kill somebody," complained frazzled Fritz. "She orders sushi at the restaurant— every single piece on ze menu. Zen she doesn't touch any of it. I hear her doing bulimia in my bathroom. She *j'accuse* me of trying to poison her with sediment at the bottom of the wine. She call my penis 'Mr. Droopy.' She hit her female roommate over the head with a bottle during an argument, so she can't go home. She crashes in my bed at 7 a.m. and sleep the sleep of ze dead. She awake at 4:30 in the afternoon and demands tea and caviar on crackers. So I take her to Zabar's. She wants the $110 tin of caviar. Oh, no, I say, you can have the $20 crab meat. We went back to my apartment. She washes her hair over ze sink in Evian. Zen she takes three hours putting on makeup, blow-drying, doing ze hair. Zen back out to the clubs for same routine. You want her back?"

"No thanks," said Sammy. "What do I need with another night of horror and humiliation."

Fritz said hello to Mike Florio, the Stud, who was also working the Mike Todd Room. "The reason I'm not in a band," he told Fritz, "is I know I'd be goin' through 15 or 20 girls a night. I like to keep it down to four or five."

"I know what you mean," agreed Fritz.

Sammy observed the Stud casting out his own line and reelin' 'em in. "I've made a study of this for years," Sammy explained. "The most fucked-up jerks are fucking the hottest sluts. You have five seconds to catch their attention before they walk away, so anything you say is going to sound ridiculous. You have to scream, so you use words that trigger their interest, like 'millionaire' or 'MTV producer,' mention a few dumb celebrities. That's why they get all dressed up and slutty and come to the city. They're tired of shlubs from Brooklyn, some plumber asking them out on a date. The media has created this whole fantasy you already have to work from. Mention the trigger word, the fantasy of jets around the world, the Rolling Stones, fur coats, coke. Their biggest dream is to come to New York and meet someone in a limo they think is glamorous, who'll rescue them from selling nail polish behind the Woolworth's counter. *They're interested in the sizzle, not the steak.*"

Sammy began handing out his professional business card. He gave out hundreds a week to girls "in the field."

"All my life," he explained, "I've tried to get girls without success. Finally I figured out how."

The card reads:

> *YOU HAVE BEEN SELECTED as a potential model for OUI Magazine. To arrange for a test shooting and an interview, please call Monday to Friday, 10AM to 4PM.*

About one in 20 might call, and maybe one in 50 would actually show for an appointment.

"The Palladium is too chic to tell men not to use the ladies room," said Sammy, staking out the long line. "Sometimes I think of giving my passes to burly Negroes on the street, with the provision they all file in and take a dump. It would be interesting to see the ladies' reactions."

I finally tried tossing out a few pickup lines myself, Sammy Grubman-style. Sure enough, the girls kept walking. "He's a millionaire!" Sammy shouted after one. She hesitated a moment, then her friend grabbed her arm to pull her along. A ringleader emerged from each clique to steer the prettiest or most amenable girl away from Sammy. "Sure, walk away. We're casting a major movie!" Sammy reverberated, as two bolted away from him like frightened does. Then two chicks in a lounge chair accused Sammy of eavesdropping. He asked if he could buy them drinks.

"We have boyfriends upstairs."

"Well, if they're giving you any trouble, let us know."

"They give us love," said one girl cheerily, and both headed for the stairs.

"Your boyfriends are garbage men," posited Sammy. He became more indignant over every fellow he saw accompanying a beauty. "There goes Mr. Bozo. I'd like to pull down that guy's pants and humiliate him in front of his girlfriend," said Sammy, voicing his own worst fear. "Oh, ugggh, there goes one, you might as well pass out."

Thousands of single chumps paid 20 bucks to enter and six bucks per drink. And every one of them sounded like a schmuck, you couldn't *not* sound like a schmuck. Even a Nobel Laureate like Jonas Salk or Issac Singer or Senator Daniel Patrick Moynahan wouldn't have a chance in hell, they'd be spat upon here. But Sammy was leading the League of Schmucks with the lowest batting average I'd ever seen.

Shark's Office

The next morning Sammy and I visited Shark's agency, Tops Models. The Stud was also there. Catalogs from the real top model agencies were splayed across his desk. Tear sheets of models whom Shark had never met were ripped from fashion magazines, affixed to walls and sticking out of files. The telephone was on the ring "from the coast."

During business hours, Shark wore his coyote fur and cowboy hat with stained bell bottoms circa 1967. There was always the suspicious air of a colostomy bag about. Sammy believed Shark wore one, but never dared ask.

The other night, Shark and the Stud were rejected at Stringfellow's entrance as *persona non grata*. Sammy suggested Shark call the crack hotline on the doorman. Shark turned stone sober: "I don't drop a dime on anyone," said Shark. "That's no joke. I don't even wanna associate with a man who jokes like that."

But Shark did associate with Grubman and his shabby model agency steered dozens of girls Grubman's way for "interviews."

"All I do is sit at home," said Sammy. "You'd never in a hundred years figure such an easy way to meet girls. I've got 'em comin' right to the door, don't have to lift a finger... God takes care of men like me this way."

"It ain't God, buddy," explained Shark. "Anyone good enough to give my girls work is good enough to fuck 'em."

Occasionally the more experienced models who came to Shark's office would stand up and yell, "Fake! Fraud!" then bolt out the door. But most prospects stayed through their interviews. Shark would take on almost anybody. He delivered soulful, eye-to-eye pep talks to secretaries and A&P checkout girls as they left his office with a printout of modeling leads— usually pilfered from that week's *BackStage* magazine.

The Stud, decked out in his cockpit jacket, was headed for a model's convention at the New York Hilton. All the best cunt on the planet would be there, he said, licking his chops. He was aiming for Paulina Porizkova tonight.

"I don't care how beautiful she is," said Shark. "Someday her husband or someone is gonna get tired of fucking her. I think you got a shot, pal."

And then Shark looked me over, as I was initiated into the club. "You wanna gamble with top models," he said, "you get bigger payoffs, or bigger rejections. You gotta remember, as consolation, when these girls reach 30 they start to fall apart, they're going to spend the next 40 years looking terrible with nobody paying attention to them. Meanwhile, you'll be on the rise, Jack."

"I take great pleasure in realizing that," said Sammy.

The Stud himself had a hard time last night at the Palladium. He denied botching it with Ford model Meg Calendar.

"You struck out," came Shark, "you hit the mud with her, buddy."

"I talked to her for 10 minutes."

"That's right, buddy, all you did was *talk*."

"What?! I'll eat her brains out. I'll fuck the shit outta her! When *I* want to!" yelled the Stud, jabbing his finger.

"She'll spit you out like dirt!" came Shark. Disgusted, the Stud downed his beer and headed out for the convention, slamming the door.

"There goes the consummate professional," said Shark of his protégé, shaking his head, bemused. "Don't ever underestimate him. He's a 15th round knockout artist. Bastard'll probably fuck Paulina, Vendela *and* Helena. Doze chicks'll be all over him like a cheap suit. He's lethal. Michael can get any girl he wants, girls who've turned down hundreds of guys. The later it gets in the night, the more the killer instinct comes out. This is like Leonardo da Vinci designing a ship. This is like Michelangelo painting a chapel."

Then he chuckled knowingly. "Except Meg Calendar... I dunno."

Meg Calendar was the crown jewel in Shark's stable. "Boner City," said Sammy, leafing through her portfolio, wincing in pain. An absolute 10, she made the rest of Shark's stable resemble, in Sammy's estimation, "a pig sty." She was a Ford model who maintained some mysterious allegiance to Shark from her early days. Meg still sought Shark's career advice, perhaps out of pity. Somehow, Shark procured Meg a small part in a *Miami Vice* episode, along with bikini walk-ons in a few Hollywood movies. He kept her Ford Agency portfolio front and center on his desk.

I skimmed through it. Every pose was haughty, superior, sophisticated. Height 5'8", size 8, bust 34D, waist 24, hips 34. She had a blonde mane teased around her forehead like a lion. But apparently Meg Calendar was too cold for anybody to *like*. Too fabulous for her own good. The only thing people viewed her as was a goddess. Shark showed a clipping of her from last week's *Post*, posing with Fabio, her male counterpart, at the Palladium. If a cartoon thinking balloon were to accompany the photo, it would say, "Don't even *think* about it, Fab."

"Diz chick don't need Fabio," said Shark. "All she's gotta do is stand in front of a mirror and masturbate."

"When I first saw her I turned my head away," Grubman confessed, "'cause I knew I'd feel deprived the rest of my life. Why go on living? When I see her pictures, I know I'll feel sick for years for not being able to get her."

"I walked up to Menahem Golan [of Golan-Globus Productions] at a party with her," recalled Shark. "He cleared people away and treated me like royalty. 'Mr. Golan,' I says, 'I'd like to send you her pictures and résumé.' He takes out a pen and writes down my number and everything, says to make sure I send 'em pronto.

"Lemme tell ya about diz chick, okay," continued Shark. "She's the most ruthlessly ambitious model I've ever known. She's a storm trooper of ambition. She eats up guys and spits them out. Lesbians try for her, just like construction workers. As a matter of fact, there's only one guy who might have a shot at her."

"Who's that?" I asked.

"You, my friend."

"Me?"

"You could have her. Meg Calendar can be in your bed. But only if you follow my instructions. I know diz chick like the back of my hand. She don't need sex with nobody, she just looks in the mirror and comes. She's a narcissist."

Shark did seem to have some sort of odd past with the model, who long since left his humble agency for Ford. She was a glacial tower all right, and wouldn't look twice at another human being unless they were an A-list movie director. Yet she still called him, the lowest modeling agent in New York, even had lunch with him between $10,000 assignments.

"Lemme tell ya 'bout diz chick. She pisses ice water. I know guys with a little money who hang around model agencies, lookin' to take 'em out. They don't even try. Meg is high-stakes poker, pal. You're playin' cards with Amarillo Slim. You'll never be the one to fuck her. She'll fuck you."

"Literally or figuratively?"

"Both... Okay, lemme tell ya how ya gotta deal with diz chick," said Shark. His voice lowered, as if imparting the most classified military instructions. "Ya gotta bullshit a little the first time, it's the only way one of dese models will see ya. Do you have any movie contacts we could start with?"

As a matter of fact I had, sort of. For starters, a couple of old friends up at *Saturday Night Live*. I occasionally attended rehearsals. In a few weeks the guest host was going to be Francis Ford Coppola.

"Francis?" said Shark. "That's perfect! She'd kill to be in one of his movies. I'll call her right away."

Shark called Meg on the spot, told her he's got this good friend he'd like to fix her up with who's tight with *SNL*. He said who the guest host was going to be and that the friend could bring her up to rehearsals in a few weeks, introduce her to Francis, then maybe attend the cast party after the show airs.

"You're rollin', buddy," said Shark, hanging up the phone. "When you meet her, just tell her *Francis*," he instructed. "Don't even say his last name. She'll know Francis. If you say his last name, you'll blow the whole deal. You let her meet Francis, get a few drinks into diz bitch, don't take much to get 'er drunk, and buddy, she'll fuck you so long and hard you'll have to fight your way up for air. I won't even hear back from you for weeks, you'll be so busy. She's got Beatty, Nicholson, Michael Douglas callin' her every day, desperate to get in her pants. None of 'em scored. But they ain't no match for you, Josh, so long as you follow what I say."

Sammy had been speechless but now felt compelled to offer his own expertise. "Ya gotta pretend you do this every day at *Saturday Night Live*," he coached. "Like it's nothing, you're a big shot."

"Remember," said Shark, "all she wants is to become a movie star."

"And if she gets it, then what's she gonna do?"

"That's a philosophical question," replied the wizened model agent.

Sammy's Office

In Sammy's universe, he faced opposition on three fronts: Women Against Pornography; lawsuits from enraged parents of wayward girls who'd come to New York to do porn; and Stephanie Mason, his stiffest competition, who edited a handful of fetish publications. At this moment, they were both working for the same company.

"I hate her," said Sammy of the tall female editor down the hall. They competed for girls. They sent jailbait prospects each other's way. They were both out to sink each other's ships. Stephanie was a master pornographer, also considered a goddess by many admirers. A witch at getting girls *nekkid*. A female Svengali at the seduction game necessary to keep the pipeline of puss happening. (Which paid most gals, incidentally, a measly few hundred bucks per photo shoot.) She had a greater grasp of the male sexual point of view than any man in the business and could hold her own with any misogynist.

"Check out this cover shot," said Stephanie, behind her desk. She displayed one of her ass magazines featuring the derrière of an aging porn starlet. She opened the photo spread. "Look how her asshole remains perfectly clefted, which is amazing considering the multitudes who've fucked her up the butt," observed Stephanie, with scientific detachment. "And she never needed lubricant. I asked how she did this and she said it was just natural excitement. She gets wet there."

Half Amazon, half intellectual, Mason oversaw five titles a month, each a masturbatory bible for a different fetish. Current mags she edited catered to asshole obsessions, fake jailbait and feet.

"I won't run photos like these," she said, scrupling at a box of color slides on the desk. "I showed them to a proctologist friend of mine. He explained the girl, who's a crack addict, had a prolapsed anus. A very bad trend in the industry."

Stephanie Mason's girlie copy resounded with psychodrama. The fantasy personalities she bestowed upon photos of unwitting nude models were sweet, sticky, psychodramatic and charged with girlie frustrations. ("Hi, my name is Linda, and I love going around sucking out used scumbags.") It's speculated that several young lovelies committed suicide as a result of reading their own girlie copy.

Stephanie presented a vibrating plastic tongue. She sent out dozens of them as Christmas favors to older fans, whose own tongues had perhaps lost steam. She loved awkward proletarian porn, amateur Kodak moments from heartland Americans who fell for the porn hack con. She received hundreds of letters. She opened every one, her favorite part of the job.

"Look at this one," she said, unfolding a letter from one of her regular readers—a Queens janitor who signed his correspondence as the Monistat 7 Man. "He worships at the altar of yeast infections."

She unveiled a set of photos from her latest brainstorm, introduced in her newest title, *Untouchable.* "Locker Room Dare," in which college girls are challenged to snap one another naked for publication. The first contacts are hot indeed—two nifty chicks surreptitiously posing at their basketball team lockers. Stephanie receives the film rolls fresh from the girls' cameras for her own smut laboratory to develop.

In the cynical, insincere racket of newsstand sex magazines, run by formula hacks whose contempt for the "readership" echoes with every cliché, Stephanie stood out as genuine. She understood and empathized with male sexual obsessions. Readers were taught to wear their perversions as badges of honor, to shed their debilitating embarrassment. Monthly essays espoused masturbation as the ultimate safe sex. Fetishes were nature's way of diverting DNA from reproduction in an overcrowded world. Did excessive masturbation further separate people from human contact? Wasn't it harder to come back to earth for a relationship? These questions were overlooked, because one thing obsessive masturbation led to was larger magazine sales. There's nothing more stale than last month's pornography.

Mason was forever on the prowl in search of feet. She was recently ejected from the biggest topless bar in New York, trying to recruit talent. She asked male acquaintances at social events whether she could view their wives' feet. Would they consider having them photographed? Apologetically, she was forever checking women's toe spreads, arches, seeking sharply defined angularity as opposed to stubby or corny features. She considered her own feet lacking in angular grace. She used great photographic care in striking the most flattering pose for her own monthly leg snapshots, which accompanied editorials. Like silent screen stars knew how to angle their faces, Stephanie knew which side of her heel was her good side. She loved dressing up and posing her models at photoshoots, like a big girl playing with demented Barbie dolls.

But, like Sammy, she was also known to do subtle, not-so-nice things.

In walked Yvette Venice, a veteran stripper, here for a model interview. She sat before Stephanie's desk draping her fox fur behind the chair. Stephanie glared at the portfolio. "God... you're old," blurted out Stephanie. "I'm 32. You must be at least 10 years older than me, right?"

Yvette was only in her mid-30s, hoping to play younger. She squirmed in discomfort but kept her composure. "A lady never tells," said Yvette.

Though Stephanie would find a place for Yvette's pictures somewhere, she kept playing the cruelty card. "These must be your swan song shots, right? How many kids have you had? Be honest."

Yvette never had any kids, at least none that she can remember. This interview stung.

Stephanie Mason learned the joys of her trade from her mentor, the late Pete Fox, another enemy of Sammy's. Stephanie and Pete were once inseparable, founding several sex magazines together in the 1970s. They invented the gonzo style of editor participation.

Pete would go to work on new recruits that he flew in to New York from Southern trailer parks. He humiliated prospective models from the get-go. Like Sammy, Fox's eagle eye strained to find a stretch mark, a scar, evidence of motherhood, anything to play upon an insecurity. He knew how to zero in on a fault: "So, where'd you get the nosejob? Is your tit tuck starting to sag again?"

"C'mon, Peter, that's not nice to say," came Stephanie, playing good cop. If a girl was willing to put up with this, if her self-esteem was that low—and most girls were masochistic—Pete worked that fault for all it was worth. Of course, girls took negative criticism to heart. No matter how beautiful the girl was, if she stayed, he knew she regarded herself as no better than a sack of shit. When the recruits first laid eyes on this skinny-assed, alkie editor, who looked like Willie Nelson's grandfather, they'd think, "Oh, my god, I'll *never* fuck *him*."

Fox resembled an aging "Hell No, We Won't Go" hippie from 1969— which he was. He wore a gray ponytail, torn blue jeans, a biker bandanna. Once, when he was editor of *Outlaw Biker*, he was confronted by a motorcycle gang at a rally. Fox couldn't name a single part of the Harley. He walked off in humiliation before the laughing bikers, revealing himself as a total dilettante.

Fox's predatory talent lay with the girls. He never came on at first. He waited until breaking down what little confidence the maidens possessed. Here they were, flown all the way into the Big Apple from some Missouri pig farm at the expense of a national magazine, thirsty for a few crumbs of recognition and a compliment or two for the only tangible assets they had— their bodies. At the end of Fox's procurement sessions, he'd invite a few girls back into his office. Then he seized the moment, holding aloft several mockup covers with their photos attached: "I can put either *you, you* or *you* on the cover. It's up to all of *you*—*you* make the decision.

"Now... Who goes home with me?"

That was Fox's legacy to Stephanie, before he dropped dead of a heart attack in his late 40s. Now Stephanie ran the whole ship by herself, and was quite gifted.

"I guess we could put you in our new *Over 40* magazine," Stephanie told Yvette, finally offering a concession. "But don't call us, we'll call you."

The aging stripper trudged on. And soon after retired.

Down the hall, Sammy took pains to avoid contact with Stephanie in their workaday environment. Sometimes they made cold contact when passing the reception desk or water cooler. Stephanie got Sammy in trouble recently by clipping a particularly bad review of *Oui* which she made sure their publisher in Connecticut saw. A "horsey" woman, Sammy dismissed her as an "ugly bitch who blabbers too much."

Sammy dressed like a stock analyst in a suit and tie every morning. Gynecological slides were scattered across his desk.

"We're waiting for this one to turn 18," he whined, passing over contact sheets with a loupe. A shoot with a 17-year-old brunette sucking dildos. She had that dumb "sloe-eyed" expression that Sammy so covets—eyes rolled up in swallowing abandon, only the whites showing.

Grubman suffered a hard lesson with this exotic beauty. The mother presented fake I.D. when she accompanied her daughter to the office for Sammy's mandatory "test shots." Sammy went bonkers over the girl, got her oiled up and soon she was deep-throating a veiny, black rubber dildo before the camera.

Five months later, when the photo set hit the stands, the mother filed a $1-million lawsuit. If that ain't entrapment. It became one of Sammy's ongoing headaches, but one he planned to avenge. Sammy had a second, even dirtier photo shoot with the girl, which he intended to publish after her 18th birthday.

All kinds of trailer-trash mother-daughter scams befall poor schmucks in the girlie business. Although the lawsuit named only Sammy, he was a smokescreen for the real publisher. There were a dozen men's magazine goniffs in New York, each with their own independent second-rate empires. None were proud frontmen like Hefner, Guccione, Flynt or Goldstein—who made up the frontline, the Detroit of sex. Sammy fronted for the shadowy, second-string imitators. Ashamed of their work, these businessmen remained hidden behind layers of paperwork. They hid behind shell corporations with noble-sounding names, like Knight Publications. One secretive smut king stirred up the ire of environmentalists by building a heliport on his pristine Connecticut land, scattering geese and ducks every time he coptered in from the city.

Sammy had worked for most of them. They saw in Sammy a younger version of themselves. They would perhaps like to have done badder things on a grander scale, but like Sammy, they all lacked the balls to be murderous. So they settled on being shrewd, deceptive, eager to cheat—characteristics they also admired in Sammy. They were actually no different than publishers of most mainstream publications, maybe better. If Sammy was sly enough to embezzle a few shekels from the budget, then by God, these men wanted him fronting their operations.

Sammy's Childhood Heroes

Sammy Grubman's personality was shaped by the pawnbroking business. Pawnbrokers were his heroes growing up. His mother didn't love him and his father gave him beatings. "Not on the head, not on the head!" Mrs. Grubman screamed at Sammy's father as he flailed away at little Sammy. Sammy's only solace after school was retreating to Simpson's Hockshop to revel in the company of old Jewish pawnbrokers and their fabulous mockey cons.

Sammy's favorite memory was when a Black hustler came rushing into Simpson's demanding a hundred bucks for some jewel. Old Mr. Simpson laughed, said it wasn't worth a tenth of that. The Black dude then asked for $50. The pawnbroker said forget it, it was worthless, a fake. Maybe he'd pay five bucks. The black guy left in a huff. But a minute later he walked back through the door, asking $25. The pawnbroker, with great impatience, totally disinterested, said he'd give the guy 10 bucks. The Black guy took it.

The moment the Black guy left, the broker was on the phone. A group of diamond district merchants from 47th Street with loupes arrived 10 minutes later. They gasped when they saw the gem, *oohed* and *ahhed*. They offered 20 grand.

What impressed Sammy was how the broker Jewed the Black guy down to $10, risking a 20 grand loss. It was all a game, the spirit of it being to see how much you could get for nothing. The broker sensed the Black guy's desperation, knew he'd be back in a minute. And he derived his satisfaction by acquiring the gem for a sawbuck, rather than even giving the guy a hundred bucks, still a ridiculous fraction of its worth.

"Why not give the guy a few hundred—it would still be ripping him off?" I asked Sammy.

Sammy recoiled, as if I'd missed the whole point, the beauty of it. "The guy stole the gem anyway, why should he *not* get ripped off?

Sammy's sunken eyes were like loupes, the kind used by jewelers and by sex magazine editors who pored over contact sheets. He sold hot watches to magazine publishers—notorious old *schtarkers* of the newsstand wars, like Myron Fass, Murry Traub, Carl Ruderman, Harvey Shapiro. And that is how he first came to meet them. From selling them watches. They saw their younger selves in Sammy, a shrewd throwback Jew, the kind they didn't make anymore. They hired him to helm their skin divisions, the second-rate tits-and-assers that were last-choice impulse buys on the newsstand, after the masturbator had already gone through that month's *Playboy*, *Penthouse* or *Hustler*. Sammy would siphon off a thousand for himself, scrimping and cheating his way through the cut-rate monthly budgets of each rag. When bosses caught him raiding the cookie jar they only admired him more. Sammy would rip off a writer here, a nude model there. Just like a pawnbroker.

"You have to get on your knees to get paid by Sammy Grubman," moaned one photographer to Shark.

"Lower," said Shark.

Sammy also fenced off bicycles. He'd pay ghetto thieves $20 for freshly stolen bikes at the corner of St. Mark's Place, then resell them to shops. After several weeks in the bike black market, he learned to take apart a new Panasonic Japanese bike, then put it back together with cheaper cannibalized parts—so he could resell the bike, and then the parts. Grubman made regular visits to city marshal dispossession auctions with his ancient pawnbroker cronies. They acquired stereos, TVs, tape recorders. Sammy had his own clique of old-Jew customers, including the sex publishers, who bought the merchandise from Grubman, all of them satisfied that the merchandise came at the price of someone's loss. Sammy derived great pleasure in knowing the stuff was stolen.

One of the oldest pawnbrokers, Sam Katz, once advertised himself as "The Honestest Man in New York." He taught Sammy the secret "scratch test" for gold. When Sammy was a child, Katz took him into the vaults harboring fine jewelry, sterling silver, athletic trophies pawned by down-on-their-luck sports champs. He was a star pupil of Katz's, who'd taught him how to appraise gems, watches, estimate the worth of stereos and TVs, a jack-of-all-merchandise appraiser. Sammy appraised girls the same way—notating blemishes, pimpled asses, cellulite and future wrinkles on their naked bodies. He was never really able to enjoy any of this merchandise himself—either the stereos or the women—just appraise and resell it. The enjoyment was in the turnover, making money he would sock away and take to the grave.

Sammy was currently editorial chief at *Oui*, and the conceptual editor of endless one-shot specials. An *idea man*. He didn't bother with nuts-and-bolts copy editing. Other editors took care of the mechanics while Sammy played the field. Guys like associate editor Michael Melville. A nerdy sort who never participated in any sexual endeavors of the magazine, Melville did line editing, proofreading, took care of punctuation. But judging by endless typos and grammatical mistakes in any 1980s issue of *Oui,* one might gather the proofreader was a bit distracted.

According to Sammy, he was just dumped by a blind girlfriend after he bought her a stereo which she considered the wrong brand. So he went back to dating a "welfare Negress with three kids," says Sammy, one who stole the furniture out of Melville's apartment before she last left him.

"Somehow," said Sammy, "the Negress got Michael to pose for some weird pictures. Pictures of Michael standing there examining his own penis under a microscope. The Negress convinced Michael that this was so funny they should make prints and send some to his friends. Then she convinces him to send them to his own mother, father and relatives. So, reluctantly, he did. Now the parents want to have him committed to a mental institution."

Meg at SNL

"This is beautiful," said Shark. "'Meet at the NBC security desk,' they love those kind of words. 'Checkpoints' at NBC, that's great, ya have to keep it a professional thing the first date."

I arranged a visit to a *Saturday Night Live* rehearsal the week Francis Ford Coppola hosted. Several friends on staff at the show made this easy. Sammy and Shark coached me over the phone like I was pinch-hitting in the playoffs, coming off the bench to replace the Stud as cleanup batter. Everybody, it seemed, wanted Meg Calendar to get a good stiff banging, maybe for the first time. Then they could vicariously enjoy hearing the details of conquest. Shark called Meg throughout the day, repeating the "Francis, Francis" mantra. As if the fix was in for a part in his next film.

"Diz girlz got Don Johnson callin' her every day, Michael Douglas callin' every night, she's confused, she called me cryin' yesterday morning, wonders if all they want is to get in her pants. But now you got it over them. Ya take diz bitch to *SNL*, get her a few drinks, then a few more drinks, till she's drunk, and you can fuck the shit outta her all night. I'm the closest friend she's got, I know. Just follow my instructions."

"Make her be a mercenary," adds Sammy, pitching his own strategy. "She thinks you're a big shot. But if Francis sits down next to her to discuss movie stuff, she'll walk off with his 300-pound belly. If you forget that and think she likes you for your looks or 'cause you're a nice guy—if you let down your guard and reveal your desire—you've blown it. You're merely her liaison of the moment into the world of movie directors."

Grubman remained awestruck over Meg. "I'd be a nervous wreck in your shoes," he admitted. He once asked Shark what he could cook up to get Meg, but Shark said Fuhgeddaboudit, Jack, you don't have the guns to deal with diz chick, she's outta your league. It was the movie biz, and nothing but, that got her attention.

On the day of the *SNL* rehearsal, mid-week, I received a morning call from Shark. "Remember," he reiterated, "just say Francis to her, that's the key word. Don't say Francis Ford Coppola, that'll fuck it up, just Francis. That's music to her ears. She loves Francis, she's totally mesmerized by diz guy, she almost met him once, she'll do anything to get in one of his movies. But make it sound familiar. Just say, 'Francis'll be there.' Then call me back in a coupla weeks when you come up for air."

Shark caught his breath a moment, showing fatherly concern toward my welfare. "Just remember one thing with diz girl... Don't ever let down your guard. It's easy to fall for her, surrounded by all her beauty and largesse. Then you let down your guard and get hit by a right cross and it's lights out. She's a maneater."

Shark was spent. His work was done. Working diligently for several weeks to secure this event, he could now bow out and let nature take its course. Thereafter, with Meg on my arm at parties, according to Shark and Sammy, every big shot in the room would stop in their tracks; women would act catty and jealous, important people would gravitate toward me, anxious to exchange numbers, to ask me for her pictures and portfolio. This was the type of pimpish power that Sammy and Shark craved more than anything in life.

That afternoon, right on time, my doorbell rang. "Meg Calendar," sang the voice at the intercom.

"Want to come up?"

"No." I went down, exited the elevator and saw her in person for the first time through the lobby window. Her photos did her a disservice. She was a goddess, blindingly beautiful, the effect of which could not be experienced from any photograph. She wore what might be considered a tastefully expensive ensemble. A scarf wove through her flowing blonde mane, impossible curls bouncing with vitality. Eyes of charismatic blue sparkled, creamy flesh radiating health. Her cleavage revealed just enough bosom to inspire wonder, yet not be offensive at a PTA meeting.

For some reason, I wore a turquoise V-neck sweater as a shirt. I'd never worn it this way before and felt like a schmuck from the get-go. I hailed us a cab. Meg allowed me to open the door and stepped in. I introduced myself. Slightly annoyed, she felt obliged to mumble a few words back.

"I've been with the Ford Agency since I was 14. Now I'm 23," she confessed, with a sorrowful shrug. "I looked exactly the same when I was 14 as I do now—built the same."

"Wow, you must really be... used to yourself."

"Well, now I have a few wrinkles."

There were no wrinkles. She began to tell of her background. She was the only white girl at an all-Black school in Virginia. A tomboy who learned to fight. It was hard to imagine Meg ever being remotely boyish. However, I jumped on this odd coincidence. I'd once been the only white kid at a Black school on Long Island. For an exhilarating moment I imagined we'd bond on this. But she didn't hear me and continued her own story. She met Shark when she was a child. Somehow, her parents trusted Shark to escort her to a football game where they sat at the sidelines of the visiting team. The visiting team was the New York Jets and Shark was part of their entourage. She never knew in what capacity. But it was a special day and they'd been friends ever since.

As she spoke I inhaled complicated layers of her fragrance. She wore only a hint of perfume, but more than that, Meg exuded some hormonal charge that touched nerves I never knew existed. Enclosed in the back of a funky cab, her scent touched off sensations of early childhood when the taste of ice cream or the scent of a Christmas tree was brand new.

"Francis'll be there," I blurted out, as I was coached.

Meg fell silent. The rest of our ride was silent.

Outside 30 Rock and once inside the cavernous RCA Building art deco lobby, the heads of male pedestrians turned. Meg had learned to act oblivious. But I found the attention terribly unnerving. She couldn't walk a city street without hearing catcalls, whistles, hoots. Jayne Mansfield heard the same on walks, but she craved it. I imagined the pressure some poor boyfriend or future husband would have to endure. Meg Calendar was possibly the most beautiful woman on earth which, by definition, made her a sociopath. I was walking with a freak.

Hardened NBC stage crew—Local 1 union palookas used to seeing beautiful women every day—dropped their jaws as we strode past. A group of electricians led us through the labyrinthine corridors toward Studio 8C to make sure we got to the right destination. Every time I looked over at her face I grew weaker, tripping over words. I searched for any sign of imperfection I might focus on to dull her effect. Voluptuousness was out, so perhaps this is what held her back in the industry. She had none of the heroin-faced teenage waif look currently in vogue.

We reached Studio 8C. There was a bustle of activity. Camera men, sound men, electricians, lighting crew, set builders, musicians, writers, directors and cast members. It appeared they were putting together a show. If you so much as touched a mike boom, you risked physical ejection by the National Association of Broadcast Engineers and Technicians. Meg scanned the terrain, taking it all in and she came alive. This was the promised land, the road to stardom. Camera men were notating shots, actors blocked out scenes as grips laid down masking tape for position. Her cold heart warmed even more the moment she stepped on center stage. She began asking questions to a makeup assistant. Meg had now ditched me as her escort.

In the middle of the hurly-burly was Francis Ford Coppola. Or should I say, Francis. He looked like a bearded slob. But Meg homed in, distancing herself from me. Fly, Meg, fly.

An extra on the show, some struggling soap opera actor who'd auditioned with her once, stopped by to chat. He approached with manly confidence. Meg stood by a popcorn machine looking positively perverse. Hundreds of kernels bubbled over the top in fluffy buds. She helped herself, pumping melted butter over the popcorn with a cockeyed look of satisfaction. The extra left a minute later looking like a woeful bloodhound.

Meg and I finally took chairs near Francis. As he rehearsed some sketch, she kept sliding her chair away from me, a few inches more toward the hirsute director. Each time she laughed insincerely at a cast member's joke, or touched one's arm, a stab of anguish shot through my gut, like I was losing rope.

But the cast of *Saturday Night Live* wouldn't really give her the time of day. They were into some advanced stage of anti-glamour, and turned up their noses at models. So did Francis, apparently, who didn't acknowledge her presence. Only stagehands came close for a sniff.

We rode the elevator to the lobby, where Meg abruptly shook my hand, offered a tight goodbye smile and was off to hail her own taxi. I cursed my turquoise sweater.

The next morning I debriefed Shark, who absorbed the information like a general. "We're picking up our wounded on stretchers, reforming our battle plans," he said. "Remember, you're in the league with Babe Ruth, Jack."

I told Shark how Meg always kept five paces away from me.

"Five feet away?" said Shark. "Ain't that better havin' a super knockout, just five feet away—than showin' up with some everyday dog fawning all over you. You walked into *Saturday Night Live* with Meg Calendar! But this is gonna take a little more of a push than I first thought. What was that other thing you mentioned?"

"The cast party?"

"The cast party!" yelled Shark. "That's perfect! You take her back to that *SNL* cast party on Saturday, sit her next to Francis when he's hot off the air—buddy, you'll have her like a hole in one."

"Won't she wonder why the hell I'm doing this for her?"

"No, said Shark, "that's the thing with narcissists. She's so self-centered and obsessed with herself, she thinks everyone else is too."

"I dunno."

"You've got to get her to that cast party," said Shark.

The Exercise Tape

Sammy had his hands in a few extra-curricular operations, one of them called The Exercise Tape. It purported to be a clearinghouse for models needed in the burgeoning exercise video market. Every out-of-work celeb was a fitness guru all of a sudden, from Marie Osmond to Debbie Reynolds. They were the latest snake oil salesmen. In Sammy's case, as always, there was a small degree of legitimacy to the operation. He did occasionally land girls in minor modeling jobs. Ads for The Exercise Tape appeared in community papers and on bulletin boards and telephone booths.

The ruse took place at a respectable-looking midtown office. Sammy and his partners kept a professional production atmosphere, with editing equipment, video cameras on tripods and a white backdrop. Even a receptionist.

"A lot of these girls are great at camouflaging their flaws from 10 feet away," said Sammy. "You get a big boner, but on close examination they look terrible." If a girl came in wearing a floppy dress, Sammy instantly knew something's amiss. "If they're not showing it, they're hiding something."

A typical appointment at The Exercise Tape went as such: A toothy, disheveled girl entered who had no chance of getting a modeling gig whatsoever. She was accompanied by a short Italian boyfriend with a pompadour and a black eye. Their car exploded on the Jersey turnpike, drenching her clothes. Sammy was mortified. The poor girl was too nervous to answer questions during a videotaped Q&A. She had a bad smile, bad body, terrible speaking voice.

"Do you exercise?" asked Sammy, off camera.

"I give my boyfriend a workout every night." She was given the obligatory five minutes for showing up, then thanked. In such instances, Sammy didn't even waste tape, he secretly unloaded the camera.

"I hate it when they come with a boyfriend," explained Sammy. "It's the wrong way to audition. See the way that moron planted himself near the camera? When this happens at my apartment, I usher them out in two minutes. Never trust the boyfriends. Sometimes they bring a Negro, you never know if he's coming back to rob you. This was the biggest night of their year, those two from exit 39 on the Jersey Turnpike. They think they did a big New York audition, now they'll probably tell all their friends she's being considered for rock videos. Can you imagine the vile sex they have?"

"I'm here to do test shots for print work," said the next appointment, a tall blonde. There was a stark difference between what Sammy called "test shots" and what desperate hopefuls called "print work." Sometimes Sammy ran home from his instant black & white developer with these prized test shots, masturbating before the chemicals dried on the contact sheets. Here was Sammy juxtaposed against real-life female human beings seeking work.

But Sammy cuts this interview short also. The tall blonde wrote down her number on a fast food wrapper from her pocketbook. "Call if you need me," she said, with a needy wink.

"You're not going to call?" Sammy warned. "She's a horse. Maybe she's got huge tits, but after that, forget it. Her legs are like tree stumps, she's a horrible, sweating pig. If you don't believe me we can call her back for a test shoot, you can see her in a bathing suit."

A twinge of guilt occasionally came over Sammy. He felt a need to defend his actions: "Look, you're going to be dead and buried, you're nothing, you're not going to exist forever. Except for about 70 years. Now, during these 70 years, you're not going to have any sex with girls unless you resort to trickery, scams, deception. That's the only way you'll have sex. Otherwise you can be a good, decent guy, never have sex, then be six feet underground forever. What would be your choice?"

The third appointment was a winner. Jean Service was a pretty 20-year-old blonde, presenting a whole different picture of womanhood from the toothy girl and the tree-stump one. She listed Danbury, Connecticut as home on the form. During her video Q&A, she acted like the Ivory Girl, presenting Miss America answers to Sammy's bland questions, with a full smile and bouncy hair. Sammy was most pleased. He then upped the ante, asking her to pose in a bathing suit and roll around a bit on the floor. Emerging from the changing room, she bent down, rolled over slowly as instructed, pushed out her little titties for as much cleavage as she could muster. A slutty move.

"Maybe we should take her to meet the *backers* at the Palladium," Sammy said aloud, baiting her gameness. He hesitated to ask if she'd "oil up," not wanting to scare away this potential Palladium date. Jean Service left The Exercise Tape optimistic.

"I'd have degraded her more during the test shoot," said Sammy, chewing his cud over a comforting plate of cow's muscles at Sun Lok Kee. "Except she was too nice."

Sammy loved slimy, off-the-menu dishes in Chinatown. Fish with their heads intact; tripe and mysterious concoctions of gruel, dishes only ordered by Chinese peasants off the boat. Whole shameful plates of tough sinews, which he gnawed at, hunched over, masticating in private disgrace in the backs of dumpy Chinatown restaurants. Here, Grubman was a throwback shtetle Jew, an inbred, an outcast, right out of a 19th century Polish ghetto. This was his perfect night out. Could Jean Service possibly indulge him over a romantic candlelight dinner of livestock intestines?

And then he ruminated: "Imagine Jean Service going back to Connecticut, getting between some crisp, fresh sheets, clicking on her TV... thinking about the dirty New York Jews who taped her. Such a white girl. You could proudly take her on a date, always sweet, doesn't go insane... You'd probably have to go horseback riding, or some horrible thing she considers fun. Roller skating... she's probably got some disgusting yeast infection from rubbing up and down the horse all day. Her panties are shit-encrusted from sliding up her ass. Probably stinks like hell. Imagine the nightmare weekend you'd have up in Connecticut with her parents and the horses, the worst weekend of your life. Ugggh, forget her."

Hawaiian Tropics

A whole industry stalked the legions of blemished, fat-tushied teenybopper *gurls* wanting to break into glamour. Leading the charge were teenage fashion magazines, their back pages littered with model academy ads—institutions that used to be called "charm school" or "finishing school" in a more innocent era.

"You can't use the word Petites any more," bemoaned Shark. "The mob owns that word." The *Village Voice* had the corner on Petites Needed ads. This approach fed off the fact that all the major agencies rejected anyone under 5'8". As a result, thousands, maybe millions, of attractive girls felt hopeless. There were also ads seeking shoe and hand models. They told some prospect she'd make a great hand model, all she needed was a $500 portfolio. A cottage industry spun off each agency. There were requisite consultations with a hairstylist, photographer, makeup and fashion coordinator. The tri-state secretarial pool provided endless marks. Some agencies sent them on bullshit rounds. One ad had a talent search culminating in an appearance on the *Joe Franklin Show*.

"We pulled diz great scam," said an ecstatic Shark, the next time I came to his office. "Ads in *The New York Times* and everything." He proudly held open his ad in that week's *BackStage*:

> *MUSIC VIDEO: MADONNA & MODEL TYPES*
> *Major video production company now in final casting stage*
> *seeking 22 Madonna prototypes for international label*
> *music video. Time must be flexible, shooting to fit around*
> *schedules of recording artists. Also casting for fashion*
> *video. Fiorucci-type look needed for national runway show*
> *and department store designer. Auditions to be held at*
> *Marymount Manhattan College in the Mezzanine... .*

An old cunt-hound professor pal of Shark's at the prestigious feminist institution somehow secured the main auditorium at Marymount. Sammy looked over the mug shot of the Tops model Shark used in the ad.

"Some Bloomingdale's whore?" he asked, squinching his face.

"The criticizer," Shark came back. "Look, I make a living in this business. She's a very attractive girl. Don't get me wrong, I value your opinion dearly. But the proof is in the pudding, pal. She made $400 yesterday modeling at the fur show."

Shark had a particular fondness for furs and wore a full-length coat during the Superfly era. There were furry pictures of him in his "Russ Meyer stash," a cobwebbed shoebox storing old photos. In the 70s, Shark worked Vegas, where his sartorial taste ran to Wayne Newton outfits, now stored in the closet.

As a five-year-old boy in 1947, Shark's parents forced him into the illicit sport of kiddie boxing. It was an old Southern pastime. In his Alabama hometown, 50 miles from the Florida border, he'd be thrust into a boxing ring with other five-year-old boys to slug it out. Spotlights hung over the ring at night. A crowd of revelers made bets, sort of like cockfighting. There was a whole backwoods Alabama circuit.

"Scary as hell," Shark remembered. "And real patriotic. This was right after the war. They'd blare records of 'The Star-Spangled Banner' and 'God Bless America' right before the bouts. Then you'd be pushed out into the ring, lights glaring. They didn't have headgear in those days, but we wore 16-ounce gloves with handwraps and shorts. Then, after the fights, they took me over the Florida state line at night. The guy who ran the fights and the races was diz big, scary-lookin' man. They'd drive the boys to this lagoon with the blackest water I've ever seen. They'd tie a rope around our waist. Then we'd race from one end to the other, about 80 yards, while all the men placed bets in a hat. The lagoon was filled with alligators. Whenever an alligator swam up close, the guys holding the ropes along the bank would lift you outta the water for a moment till the alligator swam past."

Shark had learned to swim with the alligators in the blackest lagoons of show business. One of those lagoons was the Hawaiian Tropic International Pageant. Many professional model chasers converged upon Daytona Beach, Florida for this perennial event. Sammy himself flew down. It's run by the fabulously rich suntan oil mogul, Ron Rice. Rice's oily empire also had humble beginnings, back in North Carolina. In high school, Rice dated and then married a girl who would go on to become Miss America 1963. As a young chemistry teacher and gym coach, Rice was fired for showing progressive sex education films to his junior high classes. He then became a lifeguard. Not satisfied with Coppertone or Sea 'n' Ski, Rice mixed his own batches of coconut oil, bananas and avocados in a garbage can. That garbage can was now silver-plated and resided on Rice's palatial estate in Daytona, with four pools and a disco. He was also a great white hunter of alligators, endangered ones at that. He was the only man to have allegedly fucked Meg Calendar, when she took the title in his contest.

"This slob is The King of Girls," said Sammy, breathless, on the phone from Daytona. "Ron Rice *owns* Daytona, everybody defers to him, the cops pay homage, high school girls run all his errands." Sammy met with Rice, trying to acquire rights for the first Hawaiian Tropic Model Agency in NYC. "He's got this insane trophy room with clippings of himself with Paul Newman and racing cars. He's got leopard skin rugs everywhere and sits on this huge polished wooden throne like some ancient Hawaiian king."

Sammy donned a rumpled Hawaiian shirt and Ray-Ban sunglasses. 300 incredible girls, ages 18 to 21, from all over heartland America were put up at some budget convention hotel. Sammy entered the main commissary.

"They're dressed worse than nude," moaned Sammy on the phone. "They look sweet at 17 and everything that comes out of them is sweet—but come 19, they start to turn a tad overripe and begin to stink."

The girls were lined up at the cafeteria with pert nips, bubble butts, flesh so tantalizing. The air was electron-charged with teen hormones that nearly made him faint. To Sammy's great regret, each and every female prospect was accompanied by a father, or "total moron boyfriends in farmer hats and overalls." Or, worse yet, contingents of lady sponsors from their little hometowns. One of the events involved this million-gallon vat of coconut oil. Rice watched an assembly line of 80 gorgeous 18-year-olds in bathing suits dip in, one by one. And there sat Sammy, alone with his Nikon, the publisher of *Oui*, a porn rag that spelled poison to all present. Particularly in the recent wake of the Miss America scandal, where Vanessa Williams lost the title after her naked lesbo pix were unearthed in *Penthouse*. Sammy didn't have a prayer.

"All ya need down here is a hot car, and you can have all the blowjobs ya want," said Sammy. "Unfortunately, I don't drive." Ron Rice's personal Lamborghini cost a quarter-million and was featured in the Burt Reynolds *Cannonball Run* series. Rice sponsored NASCAR racers whose cars bore the logo *It ain't the motion, it's the lotion*. Paul Newman, whose motion moved to Rice's lotion, once drove the winning Hawaiian Tropic Porsche at LeMans, France. The prized celebrities young contestants "get to meet" included Donald Trump, Julio Iglesias and Burt Reynolds himself. For contestants who wanted to "go in that direction," as Rice put it, he "feeds" girls to the Playboy mansion. (Even with vats of oily girls in abundance, Rice would soon become embroiled for years in sexual harassment lawsuits from female employees.)

For Sammy, the whole trip provided another series of strike-outs. "This waitress I was pursuing at the commissary went off with a Negro at the end of her shift," Sammy sighed. "These girls are all gonna get AIDS, they experiment with Negroes and everything.

"Next year," said Sammy, debriefing in Chinatown, "maybe *I'll* be the King of Girls." Sammy was able to convince Ron Rice he was some important media kike from New York. If all went according to plan, next time he'd be flying down as publisher of a *Hawaiian Tropic Teen Model Magazine*, yet another brainstorm.

"These girls are total hicks. I overheard two at the commissary breakfast table talking about the great Chinese dinner they had last night. 'Ah *nevuh* did have Chinese.' Turns out they were speaking about McChicken Shanghai or some crap at McDonald's, a new test market item on the menu down there. 'Ah wish they had Chinese at mah McDonald's.'"

Sammy told me of his own entrepreneurial dreams for a future restaurant:

"It would be an expensive place for the rich. A dome surrounds the main dining area upstairs. Underneath the glass dome, on the ground below, is a clearly visible walk-in dirt grounds populated by derelicts, bag ladies, families on welfare. Clientele are invited to throw their leftovers over the dome and watch the starving grapple for it. Have a few niblets left on your corn on the cob? Toss the cob over. Leave a few bites on your lamb chop bone or a slice of your filet mignon—toss it over, and watch 'em scrapple. Oh, it would get a few bleeding heart protesters at first, but then things would settle down and it would be a big success."

This would have been the perfect restaurant for Mayor Koch's New York, a crumbling Roman Empire, where you had to step over the homeless on every block. Sammy's next horror restaurant would be a rib joint, where huge roast suckling pigs revolved around open spit ovens in view. A glassed-in mud patch would contain live pigs—which patrons could individually pick for the slaughter. And then, stuffed to the gills with hog, the slobs would be wheeled backward on chairs with coasters by their waiters to a scented lounge with soft music, where their dining seats would automatically recline so they could fall into satiated slumber.

Cast Party

While Sammy was in Daytona, I took Meg to the *SNL* cast party, our second date. Each week, SNL throws an after-show cast party at some unannounced locale. Two company limos dump off carloads of insiders, then return to 30 Rock for more.

My ever-lovin' darling fiancée down in Texas was still awaiting my long-postponed move there. The force was against me. I felt like Tom Ewell in *The Seven Year Itch*. If I were even briefly involved with a creature like Meg Calendar, I would dread a subway ride. Walking past a construction site would cause pandemonium. Could Meg ever wash dishes or do laundry? Could she found a leper colony on the streets of Calcutta like Mother Teresa? Would lepers and legless cripples start hooting and yelping like dingoes?

Meg struck out with Francis. He couldn't afford to be impressed with in-your-face beauty. The cycle of rejection came round. He was just as unattainable to Meg as she was to the model-chasers. Including suckers like me. Going home in the cab I entered some psychic condition beyond blue balls. I sensed these were to be my last minutes, my last shot with Meg Calendar.

"Want to come up for some herbal tea?" I asked, feeling pathetic.

"No way!" she snapped. Then she turned her head with a tight laugh of contempt.

But that wasn't quite the last I saw of her. A few nights later, Sammy and I were at the Palladium.

"There are seven females to every man in the world," claimed Sammy, watching all the girls go by. "Millions of women alone in the country, thousands of attractive ones, maybe thousands of beautiful ones. And not one for me. I get physically sick on the street, seeing legs, tits, wiggling asses that I can't have. I have to take codeine pills to sleep. It's amazing how miserable you are without a girl, how depressed and utterly ugly you feel every second. This craziness starts to feed on itself as the weeks go by. And then when you're with one, it's as if you've always been getting laid, you can't imagine otherwise, the world is right and normal. I'm amazed at these girls. They experiment with sub-racial, sexually ambiguous types, that's what they want. Not me. I might as well be that old fuck right there," said Grubman, pointing to a fat 60-year-old bathroom attendant. "I look no different to these girls than him. Young models want rock stars with long hair, pro athletes. They want these heavy metal buffoons, idiotic baboons without a thought in their heads who mistreat them. They go for oily blue Negroes. But not me. I'm shocked every day."

One of the buffoons Sammy referred to was Damien. Damien was 23, a suave, dark-skinned stud who performed at Show World. He high-stepped through the Palladium like a Puerto Rican peacock in a cheap zoot suit. He earned his living doing six-to-ten live sex shows on Show World's Triple Treat Stage. He scouted here and at Long Island discos. He laid romantic bullshit onto 17-year-old JAPs from Great Neck so thick, some actually followed him into New York afterward, fellating him onstage during the late-show at Show World. Sometimes two at once. Just for kicks.

"Of course, I gotta lay some rock on 'em first, rocks this big," said Damien, holding his fists in circles of imaginary coke. "Then they start havin' fun and wanna get crazy in front of strange guys and freak 'em out. There were these twin sisters whose mother dropped 'em off in front of the disco in a Bentley, then waves bye bye, they'll be home at midnight. These girls live in Lake Success, Great Neck, their father is president of Ideal Toys, or Hasbro or some shit, and God forbid if he ever found out, he'd turn me into a Cabbage Patch Corpse. They don't just live in a mansion, they live on an estate. They bring me into their bathroom, it's got a marble bidet, a urinal, one regular toilet and one you can swim in.

"So I say, 'Wanna go to the Palladium, Studio 54? Come to the city with me, I'll take ya to a few parties.' Then I say, 'Oh, wait, I gotta stop over Show World a minute.'" Bring 'em up to the dressing room, say, 'Girls, may I ask this big favor of you?" There were 125 old guys out in the audience, and these two rich 17-year-old knockout twin bitches came out onstage and fucked like animals. With me and each other. I abused 'em with this under the spotlight," he said, clutching his unit. "Soon as we get offstage, I go 'So long, ladies,' and pretend I'm the janitor, don't know 'em from Adam. Bye, bye!

"I got this stage partner now, I don't know how old she is. My boss tells me 16, but I say, No way, get outta here. But he says if I tell anybody, the vice squad comes up and we're all out of biz. So the first time I screw her, I say, this chick's got a *cunt*, a woman's cunt, ain't no 16-year-old's cunt. So I feed her a lot of coke, a rock this big, that'll loosen her lips. And she tells me she's 16, I swear to God.

"So last night, she doesn't show up. So I gotta go grab some girl out of a booth downstairs at Show World. Those girls downstairs get 40 percent of their booths—which could amount to two dollars or $300 in one night. Me, I get $60 a shift, I work five double shifts, that's a $600 paycheck. But whenever I ask a booth girl if she wants to do a live show with me, you can bet she'll say yeah. No one's ever turned me down. But for me to grab a girl out of the booth, ya gotta ask the manager first, clear it on the schedule. So I'm in my new Cerruti suit, decked out, strut into the boss' office, boy is he glad to see me. 'Damien,' he says, 'have I got a girl for you.' Yeah? 'A young blonde, white girl.' Yeah? 'And I want you to fuck her this show.' Do I ever wanna. I'm feelin' my oats. Where is she? 'Here,' he says, and out she walks."

Damien feigned a puke. "I brought her here tonight." Sure enough, out of the powder room she comes with a big smile. Sammy winces, muttering what a fat pig she is. Damien puts his arm around her. He turned as he left, with a humble bow. "Some things you gotta do for the company," he said. Off they went into the night.

Sammy and I entered the Mike Todd Room, and that's where I saw Meg for the last time. She walked past everyone in the crowd, oblivious to stares, and slid right up to me. Sammy said nothing, astonished. He automatically knew this was the one and only Meg. Her astonishing tits are practically bursting out of her bustier tonight. She seemed downright mischievous, a tattooed punk-rock model girlfriend at her side. She spoke. Words came out of her mouth.

Sammy leaned into me. "I can't believe she's talking to you," he whispered in my ear. "She likes you, she's confused, she never had anyone not call her back. Chase her."

"Shut up," I ordered Sammy. He continued whispering in my ear as though Meg and her girlfriend weren't there. This was the redwood tree of a girl that neither I or the Stud could chop down. The one Shark wouldn't even bother to fix Sammy up with.

"Seen Francis?" asked Meg.

"She's asking you questions," whispered Sammy in my ear.

"Francis Ford Coppola?" I asked.

Meg let out a huff of displeasure, but actually drew closer.

"Yeah, that Francis."

"Now she's rubbing into you," Sammy gasped. "I can't believe this is happening."

Meg and her friend decided not to notice Sammy. But they indicated they'd like drinks. Sammy dashed off to the line at the bar, usually a 30-minute wait. "Oh my God, oh my God," he wheezed, cutting through the crowd like a linebacker. He was back in two minutes flat, drinks in hand. Each model accepted her glass from Grubman without acknowledgment. Sammy then went to grab us a table. This was heaven—a girl-less evening turned resplendent with hot, cleavaged Ford models. But the moment he returned, a table secured, Meg waved *ta-ta*. Then went off into the crowd, leaving Grubman and myself stranded like the idiots we were. We watched them take the drinks he'd bought and over-tipped for so they could sit with someone else.

"Oh, my God. So that's Meg Calendar," he calculated. "Her left tit sags."

Adding to Sammy's anguish, the dyke bartender was glaring at him. She held up a pair of scissors and pantomimed cutting off his dick. This would be the last time Sammy came to the Palladium.

Sammy imagined a noose tightening around his neck. He started removing his tie at the office. He had bad dreams. In one he envisioned a doomsday scenario at The Exercise Tape. A *New York Post* headline came to him that read: DEAD MINOR IN PORN KING'S BED. Then Sammy dreamed of himself in a tight jail cell with a Puerto Rican AIDS victim, one who sensually picked his nose in Sammy's face and lovingly offered him some.

Who could blame Sammy for his castration fears after becoming the poster-boy for Women Against Pornography? They had his mug shot pasted all over town in their recruitment literature, along with an editorial he wrote—in good humor, of course—for a certain men's publication. He's sorry his photo appeared in the editorial because it's now reprinted in Women Against Pornography's pamphlets. He has spawned a rallying cry. Amongst the thousands of WAP's, all it would take was one diesel dyke with a pair of garden shears. It could even happen at The Exercise Tape.

Sammy's regrettable editorial:

> FACING UP TO THE PROBLEMS OF WOMEN
> *Let's be reasonable and logical, and face up to facts. Women aren't human; they're not even like monkeys or orangutans. Those muddle-headed, pea-brained, waste-your-money liberals might want to brainwash you into thinking that girls are good for something other than sucking cock, but you and I and every other sensible man*

knows better. These sluts were put on earth to steal your money; be whining, complaining and arrogant; and to serve as reasonably comfortable holsters for your erections when one is aroused by the call of nature.

First off, scientific research has it that women just aren't the same as men. They don't like things like cameras or computers or state-of-the-art stereos, simply because the higher centers of their brains aren't developed as well as a man's. Furthermore, according to a very fine article in The National Enquirer, *it's been proven that women aren't as smart as men. It takes real guts to admit it, but women are mindless creatures... Don't let those detestable, ugly, disgusting, sour-pussed lesbian diesel-dyke Women's Libbers fool you, along with their cotillions of homo yesmen. Women are most happy when they are serving their twin gods of Mammon and King Cock...*

Men work hard, make money, grind the wheels of business, only to fall victim to early deaths dealt out by the insane caprices of vengeful sluts... They should be rounded up in a pen with pigs and fucked with sticks and forced to eat filthy offal, and maybe then they would appreciate a fine figure of a man who wants to own and take care of them, even if he is perhaps just a wee bit nervous and high-strung and suspicious of some people's motives ..."

The editorial was reprinted in the brochures, though it faded out into broken type after a few paragraphs.

I asked Sammy, Was nothing about womanhood sacred? Had he a sister, a daughter, a wife? Well, he had a mother, but she never loved him. She fawned over his younger brother, Jonah.

"My younger brother, who I no longer talk to, married some ugly pig," said Sammy. "They're having a kid. He never cheats, stays home. When we were kids walking down the street, I'd see some girl and crane my neck 180 degrees, panting, Good God, did you see that? And he'd stand there going, 'Huh, huh?'"

Sammy felt some competitive pressure over his younger brother's marriage. So he decided to get him a wife, too. The lucky lady was a genteel Southern girl of 22 from Florida.

She came to interview for a job at Stephanie Mason's office. Sammy met her in the hallway, and for once, he didn't strike out. She agreed to a date. He phoned me afterward. "I just got reamed, steamed and dry cleaned," he said. "The girl blew me incredibly then fucked me twice. I'm happy."

Within two months of this date they were engaged. Sammy said her father owned a small oil company and was wealthy. "I'm 34, desperate, and keep seeing myself in my 40s, ugly, wrinkled, bent over, without a woman, and at that point with no chance. So I'm getting married."

After the engagement, Stephanie called, taking a pool of bets from everyone who knew Sammy. They were all placing $5 on when she'd dump him. Not particularly friends with any women in New York, Sammy made the bad call of asking Stephanie, his only female associate, to go out with his future wife, show her the city, take her shopping. So Stephanie, a worldly consumer, took the fiancée to the most expensive shops in Soho, encouraging her to break the bank with Sammy's credit cards. "These wives are expensive," he complained over the phone. "Mine's been spending $400 a shot on the card."

Unbeknownst to Sammy, his comrades at the office picked a week and bet $5. Stephanie felt Sammy's bride-to-be was terribly naive and latched onto him in a desperate moment. Her previous husband was an Iranian who worked in her father's oil business. Sammy proudly hoisted their Dade County divorce papers. She'd been treated so badly by men—she even had to make an appointment whenever she wanted to see her father—that Sammy's initial kindness was new to her. Of course, he would soon offer psychological torment, as opposed to the physical punishment inflicted by her former Iranian husband.

The girl had been raised with Southern table manners and she was offended when they walked into a restaurant. Only one chair was available; Sammy pulled it out, then sat down himself. She blew up over this delicate seating matter which left Sammy bewildered. He'd never held out a chair or opened a door for a woman in his life. He ate loudly with his mouth open making squishing, whistling noises. Whenever they reached a red light at the curb, Sammy took an extra step, crossing the street before her. Then he'd wait for her to catch up.

Sammy's fiancée was in for another shocker at the first meeting of his family. Seeing the whole clan of Grubmans threw the genteel lady from the South askew. They all ate with their mouths open, masticating.

Sammy arranged "How To Be A Jew" lessons from a cut-rate rabbi. He'd convert her in 12 easy lessons. Sammy insisted this was *her* idea, she wanted to convert. She may have harbored an exotic taste for deranged men, having run off to New York to marry a mockey pornographer, escaping her Iranian husband, a reputed terrorist. But she hadn't foreseen the degradation of a Jewish conversion and a wedding, à la Grubman.

"I'm going to introduce her to all the interesting men I can," said Stephanie, who began chumming up to Sammy. "I'll take her to the most expensive shops in Soho, even though the same stuff's available down the street on Orchard for half the price. I've taken out a bank account of the 20 bets in the pool so far about when she'll dump him. The winner gets interest."

Ultimately, what Stephanie was gifted at was turning girls out. She would introduce Sammy's wife to playboys and *playas*, dope kingpins and debonair blades with fancy cars and dubious backgrounds. She was dead set on turning Grubman's ever-suffering, Jewish-converted wife out as a call girl.

Sammy's marriage crashed on the rocks after a few miserable months. The ex-wife tried to ream, steam and dry-clean him in court. He faced further court battles as his jailbait lawsuit came to a head. The mother of the 17-year-old dildo model cost *Oui* a dainty dime, which prompted Sammy's departure from the sinking magazine.

But Sammy Grubman never went down like a captain with his ship. Whenever disaster lurked, Sammy was always able to crawl out of the bowl as troubled waters were about to swirl down the toilet. His attendance at beauty contests and discos began to wane. He kept to his apartment more, adding an extra lock or two and a security alarm. Flyers of his face were papered all over town like a Wanted Dead Or Alive poster. His waking moments became a brightly lit hell in which Sammy was convinced that members of the fairer sex were out hunting for his balls.

Postscript: 18 Years Later

Sometime after I left New York, Shark was run over by a truck. That's how he tells it. Whatever actually happened may never be established. The fact is, Shark is now a quadriplegic. He's hooked up to a high-tech wheelchair on the 17th floor of an East Side apartment building. Two gay assistants with Continental accents work for him. He is centrally positioned in the room.

"Diz operation is 10 times bigger than when you last saw it," claims Shark. "This is my top girl," he says, gesturing to a swimsuit calendar on his desk. "She's gonna make a million dollars in diz business. I've got hundreds of girls. Showgirls fly in from Vegas every week with their managers."

Shark's ankles are turned out at a grotesque unnatural angle, secured by metal clamps. His midsection protrudes like Humpty Dumpty. He resembles something of the great British physicist, Stephen Hawkins, albeit now with a visible colostomy bag. His fingers are frozen in a spastic curl, each knuckle horribly bent. Yet his hands, though immobile, are able to hook a finger around the phone on his wheelchair to answer. A phone repairman is there. "If diz phone wasn't broken, you'd hear it ringing off the hook all day." And then it does.

"Tops Models," he answers. Some girl talk ensues. The walls are papered with model's promos, calendars, tearsheets. "We do some wonderful things here," Shark tells me. He has a relative who's a Brigadier General in the Army. Shark is fixing the General up with an Indian chief friend out West who's an expert tracker. "Diz guy can track anybody," says Shark. "So, I figure he's the only guy who can find Osama Bin Laden. They've got a cave in Afghanistan that's 31 miles deep. That's nothin' to diz guy when he puts his ear to the ground. So he's flying in tomorrow to meet the General, I arranged a meeting here at Tops Models. The General has an appointment with President Bush the next day. If he likes what he sees in diz Indian, he'll bring him to meet Bush the next day, and then to Afghanistan."

His physical condition aside, Shark seems more successful and happy than ever. For all the scams and make-believe show-biz, he does scrounge out scraps of work here and there for his models. He sends them to some 90-year-old retired theatrical agent who knows Joe Franklin. The old agent occasionally wangles a blowjob. All told, Shark provides cattle-call auditions for thousands of dreamers who'd otherwise never have such excitement in their lives.

Sammy Grubman moved to some high-rent real estate in lower Manhattan with a Hudson River view. When the World Trade Center was hit, his windows were blown out. Thousands of naked girl test shots scattered into oblivion. Emergency workers found body parts in his apartment. In the chaos that ensued, Sammy moved to Fort Greene, Brooklyn. Someone convinced him Fort Greene, a former ghetto, was becoming gentrified. But he found it wasn't.

"It takes three hours just to go to the supermarket," says Sammy. "The cashier doesn't know the prices, then goes back to check and disappears for 30 minutes. People wait on huge lines. It's bedlam. If these people didn't have managers or officials of some sort, it would be like Somalia."

Since leaving publishing, Grubman went into the business of "mail fraud." Fake ads for psychics, shenanigans with lottery tickets, various and sundry items where you mail in a dollar. The operation requires a "designated convict" to run his P.O. Box. This is a partner who picks up the mail: "Chances are nothing will happen, but there's also a chance you could get in a little trouble. Or a lot of trouble. If, say, an FBI stake-out decides to pick you up."

Sammy spent thousands on plastic surgery. There were complications, infections. After two years of repairs, his face settled down. He now has a strong jaw and clefted chin, like the young Kirk Douglas. He has a full head of hair, no bags under his eyes and taut, clear skin. He can easily pass himself off for a decade younger and gives his age to girls as 38. He had glamour shots of himself in a suit taken by noted girlie photographer, Warren Tang.

"I had the photos retouched and airbrushed to perfection," says Sammy. "Then I put an ad in all the classifieds throughout Japan: 'Rich American businessman looking to introduce young women to New York.' I had it running like a well-oiled machine. I'd be dropping one off at JFK at the same time as picking up a new one, fresh from Tokyo. I had the flight schedules working like clockwork.

"These girls have no criteria whatsoever to judge American men, no point of reference, they know nothing. They have no idea of social strata, who to stay away from. This JAL flight attendant I have in the house now went out with Negroes before me. As far as they know, I'm the prime catch amongst American men. They never even heard of Pearl Harbor or Hiroshima, they've just heard that Americans did something bad to them a long time ago; they don't even know about World War II.

"But they like hip hop, that they've heard. So they all come over with the same guidebook. Each one says her favorite movie is *Titanic*, as if they're programmed. They all want to go shopping at the same stores for some stupid overpriced designer handbag and some jewelry. So I take them shopping, blow a few hundred. And they all want to go to Met. I've taken dozens. They stand there before the same Dali exhibit. I ask them, 'What do you see in these paintings, what appeals to you?' And then they turn to a page in their guidebook, without a clue as to what they're looking at, then read some description and look up at me. 'Surreal, yes?'

"But they're incredibly proficient and dedicated when it comes to blowjobs. They'll spend hours diligently applying oil and working you up."

After redesigning his face, Sammy has now learned that "When it comes down to it, men's looks mean nothing to women. Oh, they might have some crush on poster-boy pop stars when they're teenagers, but after that, at bottom, they're all looking for two things: security and power.

"These Japanese girls who come to America are considered out of their minds back home. Total rebels. No respectable Japanese girl would ever fly to New York on her own to hook up with a strange man. But if it wasn't for them, I'd have no sex life whatsoever. If it wasn't for Asian girls, I'd have nothing."

The Stud did time in a mental hospital. He made a lot of enemies, just by nature of being the Stud. But he's no longer on a roll. He leads a quiet existence with one girlfriend in a place he once would have been embarrassed to be seen in—New Jersey.

Shark got Meg Calendar a double episode on some cop show from an old friend, an ex-NFL player who co-produced and appeared in the series. The football player took her on a weekend climbing excursion in the Valencia Mountains. The guy had a pet chimp who went everywhere with him, even mountain climbing. He was a well-behaved critter, cute as a kewpie doll. At the end of the trip, as Meg was leaving, she reached over to pat the chimp on the head and it bit off one of her nostrils. One savage crunch. She was rushed to the hospital and had several operations to fix her disfigured nose. Shark then lost touch with her. But he heard the former Ford model was now hooking out of Los Angeles. Ruined for modeling or even being an actress, she now possesses a new cavity on her face with unique possibilities in the hooking biz.

CHAPTER THREE

BABES ON BROADWAY

I always figured I'd lose my virginity on 8th Avenue. I was titilated over the idea that just 40 blocks down the same avenue as my old Eldorado building was a shantytown of massage parlors. A sexual slum had risen out of Times Square that held strange mysteries of women, as if a hellish Land of Oz were in the city.

At this point in history, 8th Avenue became clogged with over a thousand hookers every night. They emerged like vampires after sunset. The white ones looked like little girls who snuck into their mommy's room and applied too much eyeliner and smeary lipstick, then stepped into klutzy high heels. They were lopsided, coulda-been cheerleaders in silver hotpants. Back home, they'd received their sexual initiations from colored boys on the wrong side of the tracks. Now, many had mulatto babies stashed away somewhere. Shunned in their hometowns, these hot young mamas migrated to New York in demented droves from California and the Midwest. They worked out of the parlors, they snagged customers into flophouses, they performed in cars, subway stairwells and parking lots of Times Square.

My very first morning living in New York, I felt the magnetic pull of Times Square. Within minutes after the moving trucks unloaded, I subwayed down to Child's Pancake House on 42nd and 8th for breakfast. Emerging from the recesses of the IND subway for the first time, I took a deep breath of crisp morning 42nd Street air. I must have been reincarnated from some show-biz personage who haunted the Square in the 1920s.

I discovered another dimension to the world of Broadway, which I'd known through my parents. Decrepit tenements hung storefront signs that said Hungry Hilda, Tina's Leisure Room, Christy's Mix and Mate, Rabbit Hutch, Psychedelic Grape, on and on, ad nauseam. I imagined all their customers were elevator men. Oh, lucky elevator men. Here was the last salvation of my virginity, which I didn't have the nerve to lose with some schoolgirl. It took me a year to build up the courage to call upon Times Square.

And so, with only Roy, one of my building's elevator men, briefed on my whereabouts, I was off to see the wizard, where females would serve up their naked bodies for the mere exchange of green paper. Sex with girls didn't seem like something that could be equated in financial terms then. No matter how you sliced it, I was certain, the man had a bargain.

At 10 p.m., I checked into the Sherman Hotel on 47th and 8th, a $10 room. It was the first time I'd ever checked into a hotel alone. I wanted my own safe room for the event, not some five-dollar roach trap, where the proverbial stick-up man might jump out of a closet. I bought my first Trojan for the occasion, a sly purchase, which gave me goosebumps.

An old man sat behind a sealed glass partition in the shabby lobby. He gave me the key to room 316. Then his sour breath came through the grill. "I just saw a pip run into the building next door. Big ruckus. Went upstairs to his whore, then cut the guy's balls off who was wit' her."

"You mean a pimp?" I asked, unsure now of whether to go through with the evening.

"Yeah, a pip. But it can't happen in here. We don't allow no prostitutes here."

I surveyed my room. The old black phone had a Circle-5 exchange. A huge toenail clipping was wedged into the carpet. I placed my rubber on the night table, proud of myself so far. Between the rubber and the room, I was halfway home.

It was a warm autumn night and 8th Avenue felt like another planet. There was an otherworldly fizz to the atmopshere, thick with prostitution, female hormones gone haywire. I stood on the strip at 47th Street. I would cruise down to 34th on 8th Avenue, then back up 9th Avenue to 50th Street. It was a 30-block sweep. I'd make the trek several times, if necessary, until I found the most gorgeous whore in Times Square, one who would move the earth for me. I feared it would be so ecstatic an encounter that I might faint. But I was determined not to come home a virgin.

I peered into a storefront called Honey Hut, the windows boarded with plywood. Orange paint advertised "Lovely Exotics" waiting behind the gates offering "Body Rubs for $10 Complete." "Try Us," pleaded the sorry-looking scrawled letters. I opened the plywood door.

"What the fuck you want?" spat a bitter, leotarded Black girl at the desk.

"Body rub?"

"I'll body rub yo' ass!" she said, reaching for a bat under the table. I meekly backpeddled out.

30 girls on each block stood at their designated posts. They beckoned to me, nodded out, ate pizza, scurried like minnows when the paddy wagon cruised by. Some were sloe-eyed, acned, welted, stoned and sick. Others had bright farm faces, not yet urbanized. Men trolled by in cars, as if it were an Arab trading post, haggling and bargaining. The prettiest white girls stood back in doorways, not having to exert salesmanship.

Seated behind the window at a Howard Johnson's was a bored pimp. He was treating four happy whores to banana splits—their reward for handing in over a thousand a week.

Below 42nd Street, I encountered 200-pound cleaning ladies in ten-dollar blonde bee-hive wigs from Woolworth's. They wore gold hot pants and beige hosiery, to make them seem racially ambiguous.

"Suck yo' dick, suck yo' dick," they chanted in taut vocal outbursts, as I walked by.

"Want some thex?" offered one buck-toothed, oh-so-sincere Black girl. She kept knocking down her price. "I'll give you a *nice* suck and a fuck," she pleaded, going from $20 to $5. Then she offered for free—"C'mon, buckeroo, you cain't beat that." I was not about to perform the blessed event here, beside the 39th Street Rap Parlor, even if they paid me. But I felt honored.

My senses heightened after one 30-block sweep, I paused to catch my breath. There were a half-dozen girls I would have chosen. Yet I just walked past them, afraid to make contact. Maybe I was kidding myself. The second time around, they would know I was hunting, not just on my way to Grandma's. Roy, the elevator man, and I, had taken indecisive treks like this. And Roy had surely embarked on self-pitying marches like this alone.

I walked further west to 11th Avenue, where the New York Central Railroad graveyard lay forgotten. I passed a plane hangar-sized Greyhound depot and the United Parcel Service warehouse. There were limousine companies in the area and taxi collision repair shops, all closed. I saw several maverick hookers, strayed far from the pack. Horse and buggy carriages returned to Centennial Stables at 38th Street, where the hookers stood outside petting filthy horses after their long shifts in Central Park. Both seemed like beasts of burden. I heard the patter of stiletto heels blend with the click-clack of horse's hooves on cobblestone. I imagined myself in the 19th century. Blonde heads bobbed up and down over laps in parked trucks.

"You for sale?" I inquired of a hard-faced 11th Avenue whore.

"I don't take walking gigs," she said. This was strictly car trade in the boondocks.

Whore faces kept spinning in my head as I crossed back to 8th Avenue. Each was a fiercely desirable virginity stopper. A new roster appeared on the streets, while some of the previous lineup were now occupied in hotel rooms. At 44th Street my eyes fixed upon the classiest-looking dame of the evening.

"Hey, you know it's good luck to give money to hookers," she said, the thinnest smile creeping through her lips. Heavenly cleavage in a black evening dress, milky complexion, full red lips and splendidly styled layers of black hair. She had curves from her hips to her stockinged legs that made me high. No platform-stilt heels, dime-store wigs or hokey hooker attire. I wondered whether she was padded up with foam rubber or Frederick's underthings, some kind of false advertising. How could she just stand there without being propositioned by 50 guys a minute?

A short Puerto Rican girl in polyester clothes stood at her side. "Whaddya think, should we give this guy a tumble?" asked the knockout to her sidekick, who shrugged. I had broken through the barrier. Like a trained athlete, some other part of me took over the motor functions.

"I got a room three blocks away," I said, breath shortening.

"Naw, that's too far. I like the Fulton, only one block away. Costs five bucks a room, not including me."

"... How do I know you won't rob me up there?" I asked.

"Believe me, honey, I'm more scared than you. You're a guy, and guys are ten times stronger than girls. Even if I had a knife, you'd just pull it away and cut me." She drew a finger across her throat and made a sound like a guillotine.

"But what if you have a gun?" I said.

"Here, you can check my pocketbook," offered the hooker, handing it over. I got goosebumps rummaging through the innards. It brought back an ancient memory of examining the pocketbook of a slumbering babysitter. Inside the bag was a mess of girlie goods—lipsticks, eyeliners, pancake pocket mirror, crumpled receipts, loose change and condoms. Of the many aromas that leaped out of the hooker's pocketbook, her Chiclets chewing gum hypnotized me.

"Looks safe," I shrugged, handing it back. "But can't we go to my hotel room? You'll love it, cost ten bucks, twice as much as yours."

"I don't go to nobody's room... Where'd you say it was?"

The hooker requested that Rosa, her partner, wait outside the door, and I agreed. Her name was Sherri and she was 21—four whole years older than me, which made a hell of a difference. She was a woman, not a girl, like my schoolmates. As a matter of fact, she reminded me of Liz Taylor in *Suddenly Last Summer*, and I couldn't believe she was so casually walking with me into a sexual encounter. I snuck a look at her 'hind end, which jiggled right into my solar plexus. The two hookers and I strolled up 8th Avenue, all lighting up Marlboros. Then Sherri put her arm around my waist.

We all entered the Sherman Hotel, where my safe room awaited. As we reached the narrow staircase, a crude gate came crashing down, activated by the old man in the booth.

"What gives?" I asked.

"We don't allow no prostitutes in here. We respect the law."

"What?" I stammered, incredulously, while Sherri rolled her eyes. "You know, I travelled all the way in from Pittsburgh on business for a company meeting at your hotel. And you're saying we can't conduct the meeting here?" "Chief, you cannot bring *any* women up to the rooms."

"My God, I'll lose the account." My voice jumped an octave.

"What type of account is that?" came the old man.

"Monsanto burlap and sorghum products." Pure nervous energy was running my show. I tugged at the anti-hooker gate, solid as a jail. I prayed the man would believe me. I didn't even know what burlap and sorghum were—just remembered them as national products of Third World nations in social studies reports. Now my virginity was on the line.

Sherri and her sidekick were giggling. She put in her two cents: "Look, we got a burlap buyers' conference in the morning. We need to go over the books ta-night!"

"You wanna go upstairs alone, fine, but no whores or pips," the man said straight to me.

Sherri turned to leave. "Why don't you come down the street to my hotel. It's okay, really." I was terrified of those fleabag joints, didn't know who would pop out of the closet. But I followed after Sherri, before my prize hooker disappeared into the sea after I'd spent three hours picking her out. I even felt romantic.

"You sure it's cool in there?" I asked.

"Christ, yeah, I'm there all the time... Listen, honey, I've spent a whole half-hour trying to settle down with you. I can't waste another minute." The honeymoon was over, her voice strictly business. "Follow me."

Five minutes later, we stepped up a flight of stairs where a long line of impatient hookers and dazed johns awaited the Fulton Hotel registration desk. The johns had to sign in as "Mrs. & Mrs.," Sherri explained, due to some quirk of the law. They were then issued five-dollar "honeymoon suites," where the clerk wished them a pleasant 30-minute stay. My adrenaline activated, I began congratulating all the old gents ahead of me for getting married. The man in front accepted my handshake with a nod and thanks. I complimented the fellow behind for choosing one helluva bride.

When I reached the desk, I pulled out a wad of bills, which Sherri studied carefully. I had started with a hundred bucks, minus the ten for the Sherman room. Now I plucked out a five, then signed the register "Mr. & Mrs. Quickfuck." The register was thick, thousands of marriages puffing up the pages with ink.

Once this business was complete, I became withdrawn, following Sherri to room 27. Rosa stayed in the lobby. My next function—sticking it in for the first time in this 8th Avenue fleabag—now seemed like an unpleasant ritual I had to perform. I wasn't sure if I would have preferred to just talk.

The honeymoon suite was a stale-smelling cubicle. The window peered upon an enclosed, graying, brick-wall shaft. I locked the door with a tiny hook. The floor wasn't level, and the queen-size bed sagged with a terrible loneliness. Not one genuinely married couple had ever slept on it. Sherri pulled the bedspread down, something she did a dozen times a night.

"Wha'd you say yer name was?"

"George. George Disoto." Once, in high school, a kid named George

Disoto had blurted out my name to the cops when he got busted for dealing hash. I decided I would thereafter summon forth Disoto's name when I needed an alias.

"Well, George, honey. What was it you were interested in?" Sherri seemed a bit tired and professional now, removing her pocketbook strap from around her shoulder. I suddenly noticed a nasal congestion in her voice, and a sloth-like droop to her eyelids. I checked her arms for needle marks, but they were smooth as Ivory Snow.

"You know. Just the regular stuff," I shrugged. Sex was no longer on my mind. "I'll congratulate you if you can get it up," I suddenly said, hoping she'd think I was an old hand who just happened to call on a pro tonight. She didn't seem to suspect I was a pathetic first-timer.

"Well, a *half-and-half* is fifty," she said. I was confused. "You know, that's where I blow ya first, then we fuck." I fumbled for my bills and counted out fifty for the hooker. This was twice the going rate for girls on 8th Avenue. She bagged the money quickly, then sat down on the bed, in no rush to get undressed. We only had a half-hour, and she'd stretch every minute she could doing nothing.

She casually walked to the bathroom, picking through her purse, adjusting her hair, while she told me to "get comfortable" on the bed.

"You know," I heard from the bathroom, "you're not so lively as a while ago. What happened?"

"Well, I guess I'm not in my usual hotel room," I said. I realized that if I was going to stick in in every hole she's got, as I'd boasted to Roy, I'd better get started.

"Do you have a girlfriend?" The bathroom door was open as she applied lipstick over a lumpy porcelain sink. The mirror was tilted and cracked.

"Not right now," I said. "They seem to be afraid of me."

"That's because you don't smile," said Sherri. "Square girls need to see a guy smile."

Her observation came as a blunt revelation. It was true that I had acquired the joyless poker face of an elevator man. "I can't just smile. You have to crack me up first."

"You really should be out there every night having fun at your age, ya only get older. You shouldn't hafta be here with me, a handsome guy like you. You should get over this problem with square girls. You definitely have a problem."

I had gotten down to my Jockey underwear and sat frozen on the bed. I admitted to seeing a psychiatrist occasionally.

"It could be the psychiatrist that's screwing you up. Maybe you should try prostitutes for a while until you gradually start to get better with square girls."

I suddenly imagined 8th Avenue prostitutes and Central Park West psychiatrists as natural enemies, competing for the same dollar. Their time cost about the same. Sherri walked out of the bathroom in a black bra and panties. Her face and her skin and her curves were breathtaking. If I had seen her in a men's magazine, it would be instant shoot-off. I imagined Dr. Greuland, my elderly psychiatrist, decked out in bra and panties, and what it might be like rolling around in the same bed at the Fulton with him.

"It's another twenty if you want the bra off," said Sherri, hesitating with her fingers at the back snap.

"What?" I asked, a victim of extortion.

"All I care about is money. You make me happy and I'll make you happy. I'll give ya a good time."

"What makes you think I'm having such a good time?" I asked. She went about arranging the bed as though it didn't matter to her one way or the other. I plucked out another twenty, which she dunked into her bag. Then she unhooked the bra. My eyes witnessed two heavenly white knockers unbound from their double C-cups with springing recoil. I had never really experienced live bosoms like these—only small, squirming ones, grappled for beneath sweaters of unendowed junior high girls.

Off with my underwear, she instructed, as she stretched her own panties off with an elastic swipe. She put a rubber in her mouth, and slickly applied it during the first half of the half-and-half. I was more preoccupied with flexing my arms, trying to look muscular. I cursed the rubber to myself.

"The reason you're not hard and excited is because you have no confidence. You're nervous with women, and it's impossible to get hard that way," she analysed. I took this as another fabulous revelation. I asked if we could start by kissing.

"I *hate* kissing," Sherri said, pulling back. "I don't do that for *no* price, with *no*body. If you're lookin' for love, honey, don't be comin' to a hooker. You won't find it there... But I like ya. You can suck my tits."

She fed me both of them. This turned out to be the highlight of the evening, so far. Her nipples were the best part, providing a rubbery tingle to my lips and tongue, which I'd only dreamed about. Then, gradually, the sensation lessened, and it felt like a mass of flesh with no sexual connotation. She seemed to be in a bored daze. I wondered whether I would be enjoying it more if she was responsive. But then, I knew from Roy to try not to take it personally. This whore wouldn't be turned on if Paul Newman and Robert Redford were suckling each one.

I mounted her on top. She was clean and fresh, the faintest perfume scent rising from her hairdo. I was awaiting some sort of magic, cruising through the atmosphere like an astronaut entering space for the first time. But I just sort of swished in, three-quarters erect, no friction, lots of spare room inside. No lust. Sherri still lay there nearly unconscious, with an occasional grunt of annoyance. Then she'd tug, try to milk it out of me fast, which I found hateful.

"Did you come yet?" she asked.

"No. Did you?" For a moment she snapped out of her daze and spoke to a childhood doll. She wrapped her legs around my back. "Baby, I don't get too many nice young boys like you."

I just wanted to keep my arms around her. "Hell, I know you don't particularly dig sex," I said. "But I hope you don't *hate* it. I hope it's at least as exciting as brushing your teeth."

She pulled her legs back down and became a zombie again.

"Look," she finally said, the businesswoman taking charge, "we're about to go overtime. You are gonna tip me ten?"

I believed she'd up and walk out before I finished. I agreed to give her another ten. But I had no sense of time, and there were no clocks in the room. A loud, abrupt knock at the door made me jump.

"Yeah, Joe, yeah!" screamed Sherri. She reassured me the management was just checking on her safety, and letting us know time was up. Even though she wore no watch, she was accustomed to the passage of 30 minutes the way a boxer was to three.

"You have to believe you can do it," coached Sherri. "Close your eyes and think of coming." I concentrated, and when I finally did, it was like a cap gun instead of the dynamite I'd expected. Miss 8th Avenue Hooker couldn't even tell, so I stayed in there an extra minute before she caught on.

Sherri was into her clothes in a jiffy. I mourned each body part that she covered. The bra was an especially sad sight to see go on. The panties went back over her rump, the stockings came over her legs, and all the things I'd paid $85 to spend a half-hour with, and would likely never lay my hands on again, were gone. The average rate outside was $20. Sherri stood before the bathroom mirror, picking her nose. I felt like I'd been in the room for hours.

Her Puerto Rican girlfriend was standing in the lobby, and I followed them past a line of other newlyweds waiting to sign the register. The act had felt mediocre, kind of like brushing your teeth. Yet I wished I could remain in that Times Square honeymoon suite another few hours, or that Sherri could become my girlfriend. I sensed that in time I'd be back on line, with the rest.

CHAPTER FOUR

TIMES SQUARE SKETCHES

THE HUMAN BEING OF 42ND STREET

One night when I was 20, during an argument with my mother, I was told to get out. So I packed my Royal typewriter clumsily into an overnight suitcase and trudged forlornly downtown to Times Square. I booked into a five-dollar flophouse on 47th Street, aching with self-pity, eating crackers for dinner on a bare mattress. I was convinced this was where I belonged.

My room had the requisite crooked floor, but faced out on an air shaft rather than the blinking neon signs I had hoped for. Moans of despair echoed from other rooms, like in prison. Hacking, phlegmy throats, winos vomiting, groans of other losers in their rooms reverberated down the air shaft. I soon realized there was nothing romantic about any of this. I couldn't sleep and couldn't type a word.

So I went out for an evening stroll and picked up *Screw* magazine at a newsstand close to Orange Julius on 48th & 7th. Orange Julius was the spot where Midnight Cowboys copped heroin in the 60s. Addicts from Jersey still bussed into Port Authority to cop their bag here, plus a sugary dose of vitamin C. (The establishment eventually changed its name to Orange Morris, lowering the quality of the drink confection which lost its malty flavor.)

Sidewalk encounter: A menacing Black man, whom I took for a down-and-out jazz musician, zeroed in on me. "Boy, I've got something to ask you. Now listen up, and listen good."

We came to a red light at the curb and I was forced to listen.

"What's the most important word there is?" he demanded.

"Money?" I guessed.

"*Wrong.* I'm gone tell you the most important word you will ever know. ATTITUDE. Attitude make all the difference no matter what situation you in. No matter what you ever try to do. *Attitude.* Don't you ever forget it."

I pondered this for years and finally decided he was dead-on right.

I gave up on seeing my first short story submission in print, a piece I mailed *Screw* months ago. But as I perused the paper I'd just bought (issue #403, 1976), I came across my own byline. The story came out! Suddenly I felt ten feet tall. It was my first publication, and nothing since, publishing-wise, has ever quite matched that first hit. I was in heaven back at the hotel.

But I felt like going out again. I had a friend whose place was a regular late-night pit stop on 42nd Street. He lived next to Topps Bar, a criminal enclave not unlike the taverns of 19th century New York, like the Bucket of Blood. The constituency from Topps accounted for most of the pedestrian fear between 6th and 7th Avenues on 42nd Street. A tributary of Riker's Island parolees flowed from its doors onto the street. Hands slapped together in high-five drug transactions. The latest chemical nicknames were bandied in your face by a chorus of raspy voices: "Shiners, torpedoes, 'ludes, zappers." As well as the standard "black beauties, acid, rolled joints." Who wanted a joint rolled and licked between the cracked lips of a festering junkie hanging outside Topps?

Next to Topps was a building on the verge of being condemned, with windows sagging like old eyebags. The entrance was lodged between Fun City Books and Holiday Hostesses. Were it not for one legitimate business, All-Star Employment Agency, holding out on the second floor, the city would have condemned the seven-story structure at 115 W. 42nd.

My friend Don occupied the third to seventh floors, which he converted to a nearly livable space from the rubble. He called himself "a spiritual representative of Middle America." He officially changed his last name to "Normal." Don Normal.

In the 1970s, Normal found this cavern a bargain at $250 a month—even though the floors might cave in any moment to whatever unmitigated hell lay beneath. Don had a happy-go-lucky *attitude.* He considered the nightly front-door pissings "an extra perk." The landlord first offered Normal the three floors above Topps Bar, but he found it unseemly: "Who the hell would want to live over *that*? I got me some prime 42nd Street property, baby," he often boasted.

And so I rang the bell, stepped over the piss and walked upstairs with newspaper in hand. Normal was bemused to see me in *Screw.* He later got his own copy, cut the story out, and pasted it on the makeshift kitchen wall alongside a picture of his old, gray-haired mom—who was already surrounded by photos of spread-eagled pudenda. Normal himself never frequented the peeps, he just loved the neon.

Normal hoped to eventually get himself an airplane hangar. Hundreds of clothes he designed hung from hooks. He constructed outfits for strippers, G-strings, vinyl devil robes, rubber space suits, capes and glitter costumes personally rejected by prominent glam rock acts. He physically scaled the nooks and crannies of this cavernous 42nd Street batcave like Quasimodo. Three stairways had no railings; entire floors were missing. One misstep could send him cascading to his doom. Normal collected needles flung by junkies onto the roof, the way someone might go foraging for pecans. He was happy as a clam.

On the sixth floor lived Normal's sub-tenant, a bald, tattooed Nazi faggot who kept large snakes. The tenant surrounded himself with Nazi paraphernalia, but wasn't an actual neo-Nazi. He was just making a fashion statement. Normal himself built a red, swastika-shaped guitar. I questioned all this.

"I don't get what's all the fuss about the Holocaust," Normal said. "If they wanted me in a gas chamber that bad, I'd march right in."

Normal built a stage on the first floor where his band, Don Normal and the Ear Regulars—also known as Bitch—rehearsed. (I occasionally did gigs as his guitar player, but refused to wear the space uniform he designed for me.) I could plug in a guitar onstage at 3 a.m. at top volume. Normal would stand on the floor like a conductor, coaching me on what he considered proper Rolling Stones-driven rhythm.

Normal became one of 42nd Street's most curious street creatures. As he passed Topps, skells hooted and hollered, tourists gawked. winos sobered up. They saw a Rumpelstiltskinesque oddity with a water faucet attached to its head. "Every day is Halloween," Normal greeted them. Even in winter he wore gold lamé hot pants, an open vest and cha-cha heels. His feet were black with 42nd Street soot. "I like to look at the weirdos," he said. "This is the street where I belong. Main Street, USA."

Normal's right ear lobe was pierced and stretched like a Ubangi, and through it protruded a one-foot plexiglas spear. He also fit an elephant-sized hypodermic syringe through his ear and filled it with ketchup. Or he wore a silver water faucet through it some days, as the mood required. Other normalities included black nail polish, purple mascara, oversized mock sunglasses. Normal was no transvestite, but more likely androgynous, and sported an orange Rumpelstiltskinesque beard. As a matter of fact, I always thought the Z.Z. Top guys must have taken their look directly from Normal. People confused him with a similar-looking New York eccentric, the "Purple Man." This irritated both of them. Adam Purple was a Lower East Side urban gardener who carted tons of refuse away from demolished tenements, replotting the area with horse manure from Central Park. He planted fruit and nut trees in its place, with visions that his garden would eventually replace all the skyscrapers and asphalt in Manhattan. They had little in common—other than good attitudes.

Normal's tenancy was another tiny obstacle in the march of progress. He had a three-year lease and wouldn't budge. Times Square redevelopment interests wanted him out. His landlord took him to court but, amazingly, Normal prevailed in keeping his lease. He wore a suit and tie to court. When the matter was resolved in his favor, he shed the suit, wearing a pink nightgown underneath, and as his lawyer recoiled, did a victory dance before the judge.

Normal eventually went to work at the faux art deco Empire Diner on 9th Avenue. A walking health code violation, they kept him in the back. All appearances aside, Normal really was an average fellow who loved the Stones, not particularly avant-garde or forward in his thinking. I always got the sense that Normal considered *me* the oddball, while he was really just Mr. Main Street USA.

I JUST MET A GIRL NAMED MARIA

T he hottest stripper of late to headline the Harmony Theatre (48th Street's "Home Away From Home") is Maria Krupa, the 22-year-old daughter of Gene Krupa. She migrated up from the nightmare alley of 42nd Street's peeps to the relative sanctuary of the Harmony. Only the prettiest need apply, those with a modicum of ambition or stage presence.

The tall blonde worked onstage here for a year before revealing to Harmony owner Bob Anthony whose daughter she was. This news came like a battering ram. Anthony, as some of us remember, was a leading front man and vocalist throughout the big-band era. An old crony of Gene Krupa, Bob related all kinds of memories to Maria. The Harmony Burlesque video series titled Maria's segment "Dancing to the Beat of Her Own Drum."

The most famous drummer of the swing band era died when Maria was 11, in 1973: "We were very close. I was his little girl. I was placed somewhere, but I made the decision to be on my own. I always got away and came back to New York, always, always. Me and my mother don't get along. She's a Jehovah's Witness. I tell her I'm bartending, but she knows what I'm doing. My parents were divorced when I was six and my father took custody. He used to show me off on tour, in Hawaii, California. He didn't want me to be in show business. I know he would turn over in his grave if he knew what I was doing. He was very religious; we used to go to church every Sunday. I'm not religious, but I feel he's my guardian angel."

Maria began on the ugly streets of 8th Avenue at the age of 14, as the prostitute boom began slowing down. "I had no other choice. I had to survive somehow," she says of her drug-addled teen years. She then spent four years working the champagne-hustle topless bars, then the peeps. A girlfriend of hers used to bring home a shopping bag of money earned at the Harmony. So now the leggy blonde dancer, after a hard youth in Times Square, has her name in lights at the Harmony, the only on-the-level joint left in the Square.

"I have fun onstage," she sighs, backstage, in what I assure her was once the headliner's dressing room at the old Melody Burlesk. "I like to dance. The money's not like it used to be, but it pays the bills. Sometimes it's good, they tip $30 or $40 during a set, but most of the time between $10 and $20. Either the crowd is gonna tip, or they're not gonna tip."

The Harmony offers an easier life than the lowly peeps and topless bars, where girls must beg for tips, then split commissions with management. Here, the hardest thing is killing two hours between each 20-minute set (she does four shows daily). She briefly dated a gent whom she met during Mardi Gras. But now she becomes embarrassed when she encounters attractive guys in the audience and won't talk to them.

Though she leaves nothing to the imagination during her act, she scruples at posing for mags or doing porn flicks. *Playboy* or *Penthouse* maybe, but precious few Times Square maidens make that grade. "You've got to have a *body-body*," Maria says. Like other street-smart strippers here, she knows it won't advance her career in any way to do a third-rate layout for, say, *High Society* or *Swank*, which pay as low as $200 [half up front, half on publication (heh, heh)]. The only big payoffs come from *Playboy* or *Penthouse*, but even if you've got a body-body, you still need a face-face.

Gene Krupa used to headline the Metropole, now a Times Square topless bar, formerly a jazz club. "I danced there. Told 'em, 'My father used to work here.' But I didn't tell them who my father was."

Maria doesn't own any of his records, but wants to build a collection when she settles down someday. She plans to quit the biz when her trust fund arrives in several years. She kept secret about her father for over a year at the Harmony, until she found out that Bob Anthony, former big-band crooner, had worked with him. Now, Anthony is especially protective of Maria, keeps the guys off her.

She deflects many propositions and feels no sexual heat within when she performs. "I never get turned on, this is just a job. I'm in another world when I'm here—there's no feeling, just the money. You can't really dance, 'cause the music's too low. I'd like to do modern dance, like Solid Gold dancing! I wanna be some kind of star, I really do... but not a porno star."

She doesn't kiss during Mardi Gras, or allow patrons to paw anything other than her knockers. "I'm scared. I go to a gynecologist once a month. If customers look clean, during Mardi Gras, *sometimes* I'll let them suck my tits, but rarely. If they try to go underneath, I slap them. I don't know where their fingers have been. 'Just touch me here, that's it,'" she explains, mammary-wise, "and I don't even like that. Then they complain because they can't do anything else. I say, 'You can't even buy *Playboy* for a dollar, you spend three and all you get is pictures. Here you get to touch a girl for a lousy dollar.'

"When I'm 60," says Maria, 'if I don't look good anymore, I'll pay money to get laid. I'll take a young guy out, think nothin' of it. As long as I'm not married... But now—I'm still just a baby.'"

—1985

(Not long after this interview, Maria Krupa died of a heroin overdose sitting on a barstool in Times Square. The other strippers at the bar immediately ran off so they wouldn't be questioned.)

PUS AND GLORY

Manny Rosen, former featherweight contender, is a fixture and house confidant of the Harmony burlesque theater. Holding court amongst the old dukes in the back office, Rosen recounted a few highlights from his 76 years—engaging tales of near-glory, successes denied him, incredibly enough, by the appearance of a terrible returning *pus infection*. Herein, one such tale, ending in an incredible explosion of pus:

"I never fought amateur, I went right into pro. You know, I was raised in East Harlem, with all the real tough guys. I went to Grub's Gym to learn how to box, and when I first started I couldn't use the left, so they tied my right hand behind my back. For two weeks, I used to come, my mother'd say, 'Mendolin, eat something.' I'd say, 'Ma, I don't feel like eatin'.' My jaws were hurt. But that's how I learned to use the left, which became just as great as the right. In those days, before you could fight for the championship, you hadda have at least 40, 50 fights. Today they fight for the championship, they get one-and-a-half million dollars. I fought ten rounds, I got $1,000, I thought I was doin' great.

"My first pro fight was at the Commonwealth Sporting Club on 135th Street. They gave me the national amateur champ, fella named Jackie Schwartz. He had ten professional fights. They told me in the corner, watch out, he's got a terrific jab. I stepped out, he jabbed me about six times, and I let go with a left and a right and knocked him out, one minute and seven seconds. If I didn't have the gloves on, I would have scratched my head, I was so amazed.

"My prime years were 1928–1930. Joe Gould used to manage me; he had Braddock. Doc Robb was my trainer. He was deaf, but he was one of the greatest trainers of all time; he trained Benny Leonard, Gene Tunney. I was supposed to fight Al Singer for the championship in two days. I had an infected wisdom tooth. So Slapsie Maxie [Rosenbloom] took me across the street to Mount Sinai Hospital, where Professor Berg operated on me. He took out about a glass of pus, it was seepin' down my throat. He told me, 'Manny, if it wasn't for your wonderful condition and fighting spirit, you'd never have pulled through.' I had a beautiful day-and-night nurse, she used to give me massages. I got a hard-on and says to myself, 'Oh, I'm gonna get well.'

"I laid off a year, then had 12 more fights, won 'em all. Then I was training at Stillman's Gym, my nose was bleeding. They pulled the gloves off. I didn't think, like a dummy. The blood coagulated. So I went to pick the nose and my face filled up with pus. Just like the Admiration Cigars subway advertisements years ago, the guy's big face. So, I laid off and went in the delicatessen business. I worked at the Stage Deli for 32 years. You think it was a steady job?"

Manny took a call from the payphone. When he returned he said, "I got two gorgeous young broads in my apartment waiting for me. I got the refrigerator stuffed with food, and one calls to say she's hungry." He took out a Polaroid from his wallet. It was a picture of a stunning blonde, standing naked with Manny before an open, stuffed refrigerator door in his apartment.

—1983

A WORKING ACT

There are still anachronisms left in Times Square. One of them is Harold Smith, who at 81 is the oldest quarter cashier in the neighborhood. Stationed by the Skee-Ball lanes in the Playland at 1485 Broadway, between 42nd & 43rd Streets (site of the I.D. Girls), Harold has dispensed coupons and change for 13 years. But more noteworthy was his career beforehand. He was a featured attraction at Hubert's Museum and Flea Circus, the legendary pits of showbiz, which thrived for five decades in the location that now festers as Peepland, at 228 W. 42nd.

Harold played songs on the tops of glasses most of his life. "When I was on Kate Smith's show, I remember, I played 'Moonlight and Roses,' 'Waiting for the Sunrise,' and 'Anchors Aweigh.' There were so many different songs, I guess hundreds. I once studied music, but I didn't need it for that. I played glasses by ear."

Harold began as a youth tapping the glasses with spoons, then developed his own technique of rubbing the rims with his index fingers. You need to keep your hands clean.

"They've got to be crystal glasses. When you rub the rim, you can sustain the tone—it's not flat. Then I played harmony with the other hand. The only time I heard myself played back was on a radio show called *Hobby Lobby*. It sounded very good." Harold possesses no recordings from his career, which spanned the globe.

Many of the Hubert's mainstays, be they sword-swallowers, midgets, hermaphrodites or geeks, left the organization with fond memories and goodwill. Hubert's ended its basement freak shows in 1965, while the penny arcade upstairs closed in 1975. Harold's heyday was in the 1950s and early '60s: "I got a fairly decent wage, maybe $70 a week. I had a nice apartment on 44th Street for $12 a week. I remember two great big girls, I think they were sisters, they used to do a boxing bout. Then they had a fella with a body growing out of his stomach. There was Estelline, the Sword-Swallower. I got along with all of 'em. They had paintings on the heads of pins, done by somebody from Mexico. They had the funny mirrors, and pictures of people who'd worked there, like Jack Johnson, the former heavyweight champion. Albert/Alberta, both sexes they called him. He was a fake, you know, he was at Coney Island a long time, they'd take anything. The weirdest act I remember was Waldo. He swallowed a live mouse. I hear that was a fake too—he had some rubber thing attached to his teeth."

(Any act with the ingenuity of Waldo should never be labeled a fake. The Great Waldo, a veteran of both Hubert's and Ripley's "Believe it or Not!" Odditorium in Times Square, looked a bit like Popeye. He wore thick Coke-bottle glasses and a tux with a roll collar that obscured his chin. Times Square enthusiast Dr. George N. Gordon revealed decades later that Waldo's neck had a bullet hole with no vocal cords. He would divert mice and other objects into a neck aperture then regurgitate them a minute later. For his finale, Waldo would rapidly down 20 full glasses of water. He secretly placed a rubber hose in his neck that led to a large enema bag strapped around his waist.

"One afternoon [in the 1940s] I caught Waldo emptying his enema bag in the men's room," writes Dr. Gordon. "He had forgotten to close the toilet stall door. Caught with his pants down, so to speak, Waldo showed me the gaping hole in his neck... he couldn't talk and apparently didn't understand English. He simply pointed and smiled. 'Nice hole,' I said.")

Harold Smith performed on glasses at Ringling Bros. Circus before Hubert's. He toured every state in America in the circus sideshow with fat people, thin ones, midgets and giants. "I was what they call a 'working act.' [As opposed to freaks.] The fat people all died. We also had a snake girl at Hubert's who'd let you pet the python. She just died. I still see Presto the Magician once in a while; he goes to Alaska to work. Andy Potato Chips, the Midget, he's a Jehovah's Witness in Florida; he preaches on the street. The only one I keep up with is The Thin Man, out on Long Island. He broke his hip. He weighed about 90 pounds, I guess, at over six feet tall. Most of the rest are dead now. Oh, I do hear from the armless and legless girl, she's in California."

Harold's friend, Professor Roy Heckler, who ran the fabled Flea Circus at Hubert's for 30 years, passed away five years ago in Florida.

The original owners of the Playland where Harold is stationed, Sehoark & Schaffer, once owned six Playlands. They sold all but this one. Only three such old-time rumpus parlors remain in Times Square. Most customers playing games here seem to be delinquent adults in their late 20s and 30s. According to Harold, the highest Skee-Ball scorer, some years back, was a guy named Tarzy, used to score 450. He doesn't come in anymore, but then, Skee-Ball will soon be obsolete in Manhattan after this Playland closes.

"I give it about a year," says mild-mannered Harold Smith, at home amid the shrieking, zinging game machines and target-shooting sirens. "I feel bad because people like it. This has been here 50 years, you know, so I'm sorry. It burnt down 12 years ago, right to the bottom. It took a year to build it back up. I'd probably be ready to retire in a year, anyway. But as long as they stay here, I'll stay."

—1986

CHAPTER FIVE

MEMORIES OF *SCREW*

More than several milestones in my life occurred during my tenure at *Screw*. Some of these events may sound like a fairy tale, but they are true. First, I met my wife through the window of the 11th floor, when she was staying at the Markle—run by the Salvation Army for young Southern women attending school in New York. Secondly, I met my best friend, Richard Jaccoma, at *Screw*. I published my first story there at age 20, and soon after, the first comic strips with my brother Drew; the Friedman Bros. soon became the most feared cartoonists in New York. And finally, through the entrée of my *Screw* press pass, the hot gates of Times Square opened before me. This culminated in my 1986 book, *Tales of Times Square*.

My first month or two at *Screw* was miserable. I had vied for a writing job at *Saturday Night Live*, and attended their pre-season meetings. When it fell through, the opening at *Screw* (to replace the brilliant J.J. Kane—now reviewing movies for the *Daily News* as The Phantom of the Movies) seemed like a pitiful consolation. But I needed a job. Shortly after I arrived, John Lennon was assassinated. But when Richard Jaccoma appeared as Managing Editor things started to soar.

I was 24, with privileged access to gorgeous, albeit demented, young porn starlets. There was no such thing as AIDS. *Saturday Night Live*, by comparison, went through its most disastrous season, its emasculated staff swamped in failure. But *Screw* offered a fascinating underworld, New York's avant-garde during those last few precious years of the great sexual revolution.

Our crack editorial team galvanized when Jaccoma hired Gil Reavill, who'd just arrived from the Midwest. How a corn-fed Midwesterner adopted the Goldstein persona, as his ghostwriter for 15 years, was uncanny. Sydney, our editorial assistant, another Jaccoma hire, was a gorgeous Creole girl. She would brave catcalls and lewd propositions during her walk along 14th Street each morning, until she reached the sanctuary of *Screw*. After an afternoon he spent observing us, Philip Roth labeled us "nine-to-five anarchists."

The first time I entered the offices of *Screw* was in 1977. Oddly, the editors were all huddled around a telescope. There were stacks of hardcore stock shots, dildos littered about the floor, 8 mm porn loops and magazines piled everywhere. But the three editors paid me no mind as I walked in, and fought like schoolboys for the scope view. 50 blocks away, a girl lay on a roof sunbathing topless.

Everything about *Screw* was the opposite of what outsiders might imagine. It was the only magazine out of dozens where I freelanced whose editors dealt straight, looked you in the eye and handled your work respectfully. It was the only men's magazine that paid like clockwork. The scale was low, but freelancers got paid from the same revolving two-week payroll as staffers.

Goldstein was the only man alive who could legitimately claim hookers as tax write-offs. Likewise, *Screw* reporters were reimbursed or fronted petty cash for research in the field, like peeps and whorehouses. Before I took over the Naked City listings, I was a stringer. *Screw*'s comptroller, Philip Eisenberg, was a Soviet bureaucrat who kept Goldstein's tax ledgers neat as a Torah scroll. He was also in charge of expenses. When someone needed petty cash for undercover reviews, Philip counted it out as if he were donating blood. "Nothing more than a handjob," he'd soberly remind you.

In the late '70s, however, New York boasted a dozen spectacular "leisure spas," which were theme park whorehouses, like Tahitia and Caesar's Retreat. The managers would routinely comp the guy from *Screw*. The girls were spectacular, about 20 lined up as you walked in. The boss would let you to pick out any two you desired, each one of *Penthouse* caliber, then whisper instructions for them to give their best, he's the man from *Screw*. You were given a palatial suite for a few hours, a Vegas recreation of Caesar's bedroom or a Tahitian paradise.

When I was editing the Naked City listings, I farmed out a lot to other stringers. Believe it or not, you could even grow weary of sex joints. But the leisure spas were so much fun that the city of New York closed them all down.

Jaccoma and I were also responsible for overseeing *Midnight Blue*. We'd planned to shoot mock interview vignettes of Goldstein and budding starlet Veronica Hart, whose porno film acting remains unsurpassed to this day. I was smitten. I wrote some sketches and personally delivered them, along with flowers, to her loft, hoping to do a little "pre-production" work.

Veronica was new to Manhattan and had just returned from a tough day on the set. She sat down in the kitchen and began to luxuriously brush her hair and unwind. She began to blush while describing the leading man's attempt to keep his dick in her ass, but it kept popping out and they had to keep reshooting. Just another nine-to-five workday.

"Here, let me," I said, reaching for the brush.

She pulled back, slapping my hand. "What are you doing?" she said. "You know, I thought were friends." She could handle the task herself, thank you, and mentioned her fiancée, a cameraman whom I believe shot some of her films, would soon be home. This was a monogamous woman. Encountering porn actresses with prudish behavior was always jarring.

Most women were fascinated, after an obligatory snicker, to hear you were an editor at *Screw*. They would often confide something sexual. A whole courtroom would burst out laughing during jury duty, when you were asked what your job was. But not everybody approved.

A hardboiled newspaper reporter who'd gone to college with my father took me out to dinner. "I'm ashamed of you, Josh," he confided over drinks. "Aren't you ashamed to work there? You'll never be able to get a job at the *Daily News*. You need to do a few stories for *New York* or the *Voice*, sweep all that dirty crap away."

And then, out the side of his mouth: "Geeze, I bet you meet some broads there. Whaddya say, me and you, we take on a few of those porno broads one night? Geeze, that Goldstein must be rich. How much is he worth? Anyway, I'm ashamed of you. I'm tellin' ya, get outta there."

In the summer of 1981, when I was Senior Editor, I began to notice some interesting activity across the 11th-floor art director's window. Ballerinas and cheerleader types scurried about in the windows of the building behind us. Incredibly, for 12 years, no other *Screw* staffer before me had ever noticed this phenomenon. I hollered out our window, about 20 yards, to a blonde knockout, for her phone number. Her roommates clasped their hands over her mouth, but not before she yelled back the downstairs phone exchange and their room. I dialed her up.

The girl who answered said it was her second day in New York from the Texas panhandle.

"Don't *ever* give out your phone number to strangers in this city," I advised.

"Well, just who are y'all?"

"We're *Screw* magazine," I said. "And thank God you gave your number to us. If you'd been across from Time-Life, you would have really fallen in with some perverts."

Within an hour, giddy college girls were hanging out of all the top floor dorm windows. I arranged dates for them with *Screw* personnel. It wasn't long before I became a regular "gentleman caller" at the waiting area in the quaint lobby of the Markle Evangeline Hall on 13th Street. Although men were strictly forbidden beyond this point, I was soon known by Major Anderson, the Salvation Army *commandant*. I enjoyed breakfast in the Markle cafeteria, just me and 500 nymphs in their morning bathrobes. In a *coup de grace*, the girls snuck me upstairs to the dorms, where I hid in their bunk beds. (Even the *Screw* press pass couldn't deliver like this!). The female hormones were so prevalent in these halls that hundreds of young ladies experienced their menstrual cycles simultaneously. When outside girlfriends visited at that time of the month, they too automatically began their periods. I dare say, the female hormones were so fragrant, I almost began to menstruate.

"It's the mother lode," gasped the editor of *High Society*, as word quickly spread throughout the men's magazine world. But I protected the girls from such swine: *Screw*, and only *Screw* would be the Markle Evangeline Hall's official male fraternity. Even the geeks from *Midnight Blue* on the 4th floor nearly ruined everything, exposing themselves like mongoloid idiots before our magic window.

Several elderly men also resided at the Markle. The qualifying age for men was a mere 55. In the Salvation Army's world, gentlemen over 55 couldn't possibly be a threat to young girls, and indeed, the few living there were retired clergymen types, fuddy duds. The Markle was oblivious to the impending possibility that Al Goldstein himself would soon qualify (which I never told Al, for fear he *would* move in).

Larry Flynt's charades always seemed minuscule, pale imitations of the great Goldstein. Al feared no man alive (save for perhaps gangster John Gotti, and gay power broker/attorney Roy Cohn, who represented his third wife in their divorce). During a street confrontation one evening, as we led a Times Square tour for visiting ladies, Al cut down some porn store goons whom I thought were about to stomp us. Goldstein stood fearless before their threats, said he would see them dead first. They backed down, contritely apologizing. Though I witnessed some of Al's grand achievements, it's the little things that stand out. Like the time Annette Haven came up for her interview. She was in her prime and generated awe over the fact that such a stunning creature would actually do hardcore (and nothing but hardcore—she loathed "nudie-cutie" stuff). She was a woman of principle with a sexual mission. Goldstein had a mission too, and spent most of the interview whining for a blowjob.

"Oh, Al," she would say, bemused. But Goldstein wouldn't let up, as if begging for his life. If he landed a part in one of her movies, could he have one? No, she declared, that would be too contrived. And not for any amount of money. She liked Al but wouldn't do it as a matter of principle. I'd never seen a human being grovel to that degree. He followed her on his knees to the elevator, and onto 14th Street, until her limousine door slammed. He yelled after the limo for her to make an old Jewish man die happy. It was a heroic failure.

The Great Pornographer suffered grand excesses. Several donut shops along 14th Street were actually paid off to refuse Goldstein service. I believe one shop was bribed to lock their door, should Goldstein come a-knockin'. Sort of like the Wolfman begging his neighbors to keep their doors locked at night, no matter how much he howled. Al's four secretaries received calls from donut proprietors when Goldstein went off the deep end, swallowing donuts by the baker's dozen. All four secretaries from the 4th-floor business office at Milky Way would have to dash over and coax him out. Sort of like farm hands herding a berserk prize hog back into its corral.

We did theme issues with cover lines that screamed Armageddon & Dingleberries, or Voodoo & Vomit. Piled high at newsstands right alongside the *New York Post*, we knew millions of New Yorkers had a chance of at least *seeing* the cover lines. Goldstein might complain whenever we got too cerebral, like Gil Reavill's bogus Goldstein interview with Hitler's Third Reich architect, Albert Speer, which many people believed. "This is not a college paper!" bellowed Goldstein. "Get back to fuck shots!"

A particular brainchild of mine was our Sex and Diarrhea issue. Every page covered some form of shit. Goldstein was scheduled to appear on BBC radio in London, where he hoped to score a distribution deal. As with any business trip, his secretary packed two dozen of that week's issue.

I heard the BBC radio tapes, one appalled British interviewer after another. "Mr. Goldstein, if this is a sex periodical, how come every single page has defecation, feces or diarrhea?"

Al grabbed the paper and was himself surprised to see the Sex & Diarrhea cover theme. BBC hosts raged on: "Mr. Goldstein, you are a revolting man. Get out of this studio! Get out of this country!" The business trip was cut short.

Though he was like a "Gandhi with his dick out," Goldstein liked to say that if he were assassinated, they could fill up Yankee Stadium with suspects. He even went on TV in Southern California, daring rednecks to get out their rifles and take their best shot. Californians were so inept, he said, they couldn't possibly shoot straight. There were alternate print crews at the plant were *Screw* was printed. When the Pope issue came out, Catholic pressmen walked off. But backup crews of blacks, Puerto Ricans, Polish, Italian or Jewish pressman stood at the ready, to fill in for any offended ethnic group.

I have but one remaining Times Square "mole," to this day. Uncle Lou, the beloved chauffeur, who's driven hundreds of porn stars to their club dates. He still calls me in Texas in the wee hours with news from Show World. Doesn't quite believe that I left the beat 12 years ago.

Lou befriends strippers for life, remaining loyal long after other fans have abandoned them. I once went to dinner in Times Square with Uncle Lou, who brought along a depressed, overweight ex-stripper. When she went for the powder room, he leaned over and said out the side of his mouth, "If you play your cards right, you got a shot with her."

"But I don't want a shot with her," I said.

"I think she likes ya," Lou continued, "she likes ya 'cause you don't come on like gangbusters."

Even if she'd been smashing, I've long since left the life. I married the girl who first answered the phone at the Markle. Followed her back to Texas, where we reside in a palace in Dallas.

—1998

CHAPTER SIX

THE RISE AND FALL OF AL GOLDSTEIN

Mr. Freedom of Speech

We called him The Great One. Every Friday afternoon he came up to the 11th-floor editorial offices to check *Screw*'s bluelines before we went to press. Managing Editor Richard Jaccoma got the call from the 4th floor that he was on his way. Jaccoma would scurry from room to room like a headless chicken, trumpeting the emperor's arrival. He did this in the voice of Indian peasant boy Sabu, rolling his R's: "De Grrreat One, de Grrreat One is coming!"

They called John Gotti the Teflon Don when charges didn't stick. But Goldstein was the Teflon Pornographer. He weathered 19 arrests in the late 60s, petty arrests, not righteous ones, when they busted blind news dealers for selling *Screw*. Weekends and overnighters in Riker's. The magazine debuted on newsstands the day after Nixon was elected President. It gave the world's oldest profession its first advertising medium and enabled the man on the street to get laid within an hour. It also made enemies fast. Goldstein was once arrested eight hours after grafting Mayor Lindsay's head on a naked photo composite. A typical 1970 trial concerned dildo ads. The State of New York argued in Superior Court that dildos could be used for criminally immoral purposes.

Screw was the first to call J. Edgar Hoover a faggot, when he was alive. Once dead, everybody called him a faggot. Finally, forces within the Nixon Administration initiated a mighty offensive to lock *Screw*'s publisher up for 60 years. Legend has it that Hoover's very last directive was, "Get Goldstein." A trial was held in Wichita, Kansas, a hamlet where the Federal government figured the local citizenry most likely to convict him for postal indecency. Postal inspectors in Kansas subscribed under fictitious names to entrap him. Nine of the jurors said *Screw* didn't arouse their prurient interest. After three years of trial and error, a hung jury exonerated him in 1978. Goldstein flew his Kansas jury to New York to celebrate at Plato's Retreat, and took them all out to dinner on the anniversary of his acquittal. This landmark victory thereafter insured the right of Americans to view buck-ass naked sex—with or without redeeming social value.

Al Goldstein is now an obese, diabetic, cigar-chomping trainwreck of 66. He has faced down his own mortality many times. Goldstein has undergone more litigation than any publisher in America. He has endured fat farms, liposuctions, tummy tucks, gall-bladder removal and a tracheostomy while on trial in Kansas. He has enriched four ex-wives and put a son through Harvard Law School. He's taken enough medications to kill 10 Elvises, for God knows how many personality disorders and imbalances. Downing pastrami sandwiches and pints of Haagen Dazs ice cream, the Goldstein girth has fluctuated between a svelte 175 and an unsavory 350 pounds, which he is now.

But Al Goldstein's court battles could endow an entire law library. Leaf through the annals of *Screw*'s legal history and you will be amazed by the rogues gallery of public puritans who tried to crush *Screw*—whose lives and careers then went down in flames or disgrace. These figures were branded with the "Goldstein Curse"—a dark omen bestowed by Goldstein in his weekly editorial. It works like Jewish voodoo.

It began with Mayor Lindsay, whose vice squad busted six blind news dealers for selling *Screw*, arresting Goldstein 19 times on charges of second degree obscenity. Lindsay's presidential aspirations, star career and health fell into ruin after his last term. Nassau County D.A. Bill Cahn handcuffed Goldstein for obscenity, then ended up in Federal prison for tax fraud. Staten Island Congressman John Murphy was jailed in the Abscam investigation after he fought to remove Goldstein's cable-TV show *Midnight Blue* from the air. Even those who survived the Curse encountered misfortune of some kind. Mayor Giuliani's prostate cancer was announced soon after he received his Goldstein Curse for cleaning up Times Square.

Raving morality figures who aggressively targeted *Screw* include Charles Keating, founder of Citizens For Decent Literature. The same Charles Keating later imprisoned for robbery in the multi-billion-dollar Lincoln Savings & Loan scandal. Televangelist Jim Bakker was ruined by fraud and sex scandal a month after Goldstein vacationed at Bakker's Heritage USA Christian theme park in South Carolina. Attorney General Ed Meese resigned over corruption charges after heading The Attorney General's Commission on Pornography. Among Meese's firebrand anti-smut Commissioners was Rev. Morton Hill, head of Morality in

Media—who soon dropped dead. Also on the Reagan-era Commission was Times Square's most insidious anti-porn crusader. "Father" Bruce Ritter's career shattered when it was revealed he'd been molesting homeless boys in his care all along, while squandering Covenant House funds on male prostitutes.

Corporate raider Carl Icahn bankrupted TWA and lost his chairmanship in 1993. He too had been cursed after sparring with Goldstein. In 1996, Goldstein bested longtime foe Time-Warner Cable of New York in Federal court, for scrambling *Midnight Blue*'s cable signal. Even the *U.S.S. Intrepid* went into bankruptcy the moment it canceled a party they found out Goldstein had booked.

Goldstein's millions have gone into *Screw*'s Defense Department budget. It cost a dapper dime defending the right to degrade the high and mighty, and underwrite the First Amendment law firms of Herald Price Fahringer and Ken Norwick. A model named Angie Geary filed a $29-million defamation after *Midnight Blue* parodied her 1988 Wasa Crispbread commercial. It was eventually thrown out. During my own time at *Screw* there appeared a mild parody of the Poppin' Fresh doughboy humping the doughgirl while she had a yeast infection. Pillsbury responded with a $50-million lawsuit. Goldstein owned two shares of General Mills and flew to a stockholder's meeting in Minneapolis dressed as the doughboy. He reprimanded them for wasting shareholders' money on frivolous lawsuits. Once the suit was dismissed, Al co-opted the doughboy as *Screw*'s cover logo for a year. Japanese *Screw*, franchised at that time, was unfamiliar with American baking products. They assumed Poppin' Fresh was *Screw*'s cover logo. Though Japanese *Screw* was short-lived, Pillsbury's corporate symbol graced every cover.

Screw has prevailed in lawsuits leveled by ambitious D.A.'s trying to make their bones. But Goldstein barely escaped ruin after settling a lawsuit from the wife of an assistant D.A. Her phone number somehow penetrated *Screw*'s security check. She appeared in the hooker ads "Willing to Suck Nigger Cock Free."

Any major loss could have bankrupted *Screw* on the spot. But Goldstein prevailed. It seemed God himself was on the side of this fat, Hebrew action hero whose attackers lined up one by one, oblivious to each other's defeats, only to get chopped into herring.

He bested them all. Until now. The Great Pornographer has finally been brought down by a 30-year-old former secretary, Jennifer Lozinski. This "filthy Jew whore," as she's described in *Screw*, has proven to be his most formidable enemy.

In July of 2002, Richard Jaccoma and I visit *Screw*, together there for the first time in 20 years. Goldstein hobbles in by cane, unseemly flesh billowing down from his waist. He has recently been bailed out from Riker's Island after "the worst nine days of my life." He owes Riker's another 50 days for harassing Lozinski.

"The Mafia said I'd be dead by this weekend," says Al.

"So what else is new?" I ask.

"If I get shot this weekend, you should be thrilled having my last interview."
Goldstein takes a load off his sockless, diabetic feet. "My life is not boring,"
he sighs, sinking into a chair. This week he's got a son who disowned him, he's
taking over the Mafia's distribution of his paper, and he's been arrested for the
second time in six weeks. His longtime distributor, Astro News, a Gambino
Family newsstand supplier, threatened that he wouldn't live through the
weekend if he switched distributors. Defiant, Goldstein will solidify the final
switch today. The new distributors await in another room. Goldstein claims he
lives for hate, and won't die because it would make too many people happy.

"I want you to hear this story," says Al, "it's un-fuckin' believable. I
travel with Jean-Marc. Jean-Marc is a cigar buddy, 'cause I get lonely in the
big castle in Florida. I date a little bit. But mostly I'm alone. So he and I, we
smoke cigars, we go out, we go to Trapeze. Bottom line is, he's my buddy. His
professional job is, I swear to God, he's a gigolo. He's a biker, he's got tattoos,
he fucks older women. He's from Marseilles, living in America for 22 years,
has his own home in Boca, a sports car and a Harley Davidson. He travels
with me as my bodyguard."

Listening attentively in the office are the balding bon vivant Frenchman, Jean-
Marc himself, and another finely tailored gent basking in Goldstein's presence.

"We get off the plane Wednesday, Jet Blue, and we arrive at a quarter to
six. I'm comin' into town cause I'm takin' on the Mafia and going with a new
distributor and I'm very excited. We've got four bags, we walk out to the taxi,
and three guys in suits walk over, shake my hand. 'How are you, Al?' I said,
'Hi, how are you,' and they said, 'You're under arrest.'

"I thought it's a joke. I said, 'What, are you fuckin' guys kidding?' They
said, 'No, we're sorry, Al, we've got to take you.' I explained I was already
arrested three weeks ago, what's this about? I'm with my luggage, I said,
'C'mon, I wanna go home and take a shower.' They said, 'No, you're under
arrest. Gina, your ex-wife, has brought charges against you for harassment.'"

The Great One revels in the daily melodrama of his life. Each incident is
fodder for the inevitable Hollywood epic of his life story.

"Anyway, they all shake my hand, they're total gentlemen. So they let me
bring the luggage upstairs where [*Screw* Art Director] Kevin's waiting for me.
I'm more stunned than anything. They put me in the car without handcuffs.
They bring me to the 67th precinct because that's where Gina lives and she's
the one that brought the charges. The cops are all gentlemen, and this guy Joe
here is saying, 'I'm the greatest fan of yours, read *Screw*, love your work. I'm
just following orders. We're not gonna cuff you or put you in a cell. We'll put
you in that room over there, we have to lock the door, we'll keep you here a
few hours cause once you're in the Tombs you're gonna be with the animals.'

"It's now like 6:30, they keep me there till 10 o'clock. Then they bring
me to the Tombs, I'm on the floor with 15 people and 400 cockroaches. Then
Joe here does something that makes me love him deeply."

The man in the expensive suit, sitting here as if we're huddled around a
shtetle campfire being serenaded by the town's 350-pound rabbi, is Joe—one
of the arresting officers. The detective now hangs with Al on off-duty hours.

"He says, 'Listen, I can get you a pastrami sandwich at the Stage Deli,' so he orders me a sandwich. And he knows every porno film, he's done 600 hookers, he loves Times Square. As any old hooker will tell you, cops are among the most frequent patrons. 90 percent of all gonorrhea and herpes cases come from women who've slept with cops.

"All the cops at the Tombs grew up with me. But I'm handcuffed and treated like shit. They take my medicine away, I'm a diabetic, I'm really sick, for 10 hours I'm trying to get to Bellevue, no one cares, I'm having a diabetic attack, they don't care if you fuckin' die."

If convicted of these new charges for harassing Gina—his third wife and the mother of his son—Goldstein could get several years. The D.A. decided Goldstein was a flight risk and bail was set at $50,000. After 30 hours, he was released.

"So I took Joe and his wife to Katz's Saturday night to reciprocate for the pastrami sandwich. I invited him to an editorial meeting. He loves cigars, he loves his wife, loves pussy, loves to fuck. He loves pregnant women's milk. He's a great cop."

Mr. Freedom of Speech has always worn the First Amendment around his neck like a cross to ward off puritanical witch burners. He joined the ACLU when he was 15. His father denounced him as a Communist. The ACLU once told him he gave freedom of speech a bad name.

"But the issue here," insists Goldstein, "is that I never called Gina personally, like with Lozinski. The First Amendment. I have a better chance of winning on this second arrest because I did not make an actual phone call."

Goldstein didn't use the phone, but his readership did. A full-page photo of Gina ran in *Screw*, headlined "A World-Class Cunt." It was requested that readers phone her at The Allen Stevenson School and "ask her to stop being a cunt." Over a hundred people called. She became afraid. The Manhattan D.A.'s office issued an order of protection.

Gina was married to Goldstein for over a decade. Enacting the classic Madonna/whore mindset, Goldstein tried to separate his life in two—that of urbane businessman with family hearth in a five-story townhouse on the upper East Side, with a perfectly sane, upstanding wife. A school teacher whose husband just happened by day to be the clown prince of pornography. The most outrageous smut peddler in history. Like all close relationships in his life, romantic or business, it eventually went bad.

"She didn't like strangers phoning her business school to call her a cunt," shrugs Goldstein. "So she had me arrested."

Goldstein is particularly irritated about this because he thought she was well paid off in the divorce. "The reason Gina got $3 million is I wanted joint custody of Jordan. I knew no judge would give me joint custody, so I would have seen Jordan only two weeks a year. It was extortion, but I did it willingly. What more commitment can you make? He stayed with Gina half the time, we lived five blocks apart."

After 24 years of family calm, mother and son have teamed up against him. So he began running full-page spreads: "How America Got AIDS" depicts Gina naked, about to fellate a Black witch doctor, accusing her of introducing the disease to America after a 1980 trip to Cuba. In another, his ex-wife rolls around naked with a hog, called "a dirty pig-fucker," whose "cunt ain't kosher." Goldstein pools his enemies together, printing mockups of Gina having sex with Manhattan D.A. Robert Morgenthau and Brooklyn D.A. Charlie Hynes.

It's as if Photoshop was created just for Goldstein. *Screw* has blossomed into an open book of Goldstein's failed relationships, lawsuits and personal hatreds. The magazine and *Midnight Blue* remain his salvation, his weekly therapy to vent frustration. Like Lenny Bruce, his life is degenerating into a series of arrests and trials. But they're becoming harder to categorize as trailblazing First Amendment issues.

When not the target of lawsuits, Goldstein is busy instigating his own. He is The Shopper from Hell. Mercedes, for instance, recently neglected to repair an electrical problem on his new Benz. Mock ads began appearing in *Screw* of the Benz USA president's head superimposed over a Nazi SS uniform: "Buy a Benz—kill a Jew." Rather than even press the issue, they bought the car back and paid him 30 grand to just drop the whole matter. He did. "Nobody can fucking believe I got $30,000 from Mercedes," says Goldstein. "They told me I can't divulge the amount of the settlement. Fuck them."

Goldstein is usually right in his grievances. There is a sense he's striking a blow for all the Common Joe Screw readers who spend their miserable lives in a silent scream. Surly flight attendants, rude sales people or arrogant CEO's who cross Consumer Goldstein receive stiff public rebuke in a place they'd *really* rather not be mentioned—*Screw* and *Midnight Blue*. The Curse is rationed out to the worst of them. Citizen Al can smear political candidates by merely *endorsing* them.

Nine months ago in Brooklyn is where Goldstein was arrested on charges brought by Jennifer Lozinski. The incident: He cussed her out on the phone because he had to wait at LAX airport for a rental car. Cussing out secretaries was nothing new for Lovable Al. He would rain abuse into secretaries' answering machines in the wee hours. In the morning they soberly typed up his complaints into minutes. *Oh that Al*—it's just a routine part of the job.

But Lozinski, 30, claimed to be unaccustomed to such foul language and quit. Goldstein then accused her of conspiring with a former *Screw* Ad Director who allegedly embezzled $130,000. He accused her of pilfering petty cash. He called her a "miserable lowlife" on *Midnight Blue*, flashing her address and number. And in the phone call that sealed his fate, Goldstein told her "I'm going to take you down." This phrase became the linchpin of debate in his misdemeanor trial. *Take her down* in the "Strawberry Fields" sense? In a sexual context? Lozinski feared he meant take down in a mob sense. Goldstein stood his ground under the mantle of Free Speech. His defense came up with a dozen definitions for the meaning of *take you down*. But this speech, for the first time in 30 years, didn't come free. The court found the threat a less than honorable extension of the First Amendment. Goldstein was convicted on six counts of misdemeanor harassment and given four concurrent 60-day jail sentences.

Lozinski claimed she didn't know what *Screw* was, never saw explicit material during the 11 weeks she worked there. But it came out in court that she herself mailed vitriolic videos and copies of *Screw*, by Goldstein's directive, to friends and family of the very secretary who preceded her. Goldstein turned the trial into a circus. Dressed in prison stripes before sentencing, he told reporters outside Brooklyn Criminal Court that "Judge Chun makes a nice lo mein, but put too much starch in my shirt." He ran an editorial suggesting someone "slam a 747" into the office of Brooklyn D.A. Charles J. Hynes, complete with aerial directions to the building. As the trial progressed, *Screw* ran photos of the prosecutor being schtupped in the ass and blowing O.J. Simpson. He repeated these quips on the *Howard Stern Show*. Stern responded with a lecture on sanity.

When cross-examined by the assistant D.A. about his 747 editorial, Al went into a tirade about the First Amendment. Judge Daniel K. Chun—whom Goldstein addressed as "Judge Chopstick"—cleared the courtroom and charged him with contempt, setting bail at $100,000. But this order was rescinded when the shaken judge was reminded he couldn't charge Goldstein with contempt without a warning first. When the jury was led back in, 91-year-old Al "Grandpa Munster" Lewis took the stand as Goldstein's character witness. In what was described by the *New York Post* as a "rambling discourse," Lewis was nearly ejected from court.

All four New York dailies gave him sympathetic coverage. Jimmy Breslin wrote two *Newsday* columns acknowledging Al as the media's foremost First Amendment martyr.

In his final address before sentencing, Goldstein told the judge, "You weren't in this country when I was out fighting for you—I'm a Korean War veteran... This is the proudest day of my life... Let's not forget that Lenny Bruce was not vindicated until five months after he was dead... When a movie is made about this trial, Richard Dreyfuss will play me and Howdy Doody will play you, your honor."

Judge Chopstick ordered him to start serving 60 days at Riker's.

"Jail means nothing to me," Goldstein trumpeted to *The New York Times* after sentencing, "because freedom means so much to me." He said he was intrigued by the prospect of having a big Black boyfriend violate his love holes.

Herald Price Fahringer, who won for Goldstein in Kansas, is appealing. Goldstein has great hopes that the harassment statute he was convicted under will be declared unconstitutional.

Lozinski's Revenge

It had been over 30 years since Goldstein was at Riker's Island. He takes a long pause and the tone of his voice softens:

"You can't anticipate how horrible it is. Riker's is the vilest, it's gotten much worse. I was 32 then, now I'm 66, I've got diabetes, I'm on 15 medicines. So I was put in the methadone center. I'm with 50 *schvartzas*, all

CHINA VAGINA: The Stud on a roll at the China Club, 1986.

All photos from the collection of the author, except where otherwise noted.

IDENTITY VICES: Playland, Broadway near 42nd, where countless bobbysoxers came of age.

OBSCENE ACRES: Fresh air! Times Square! Josh on Forty Doo-Wop.

DOWN IN THE ALLEY: Josh, right, on dumpster, detail for *Screw*, with Annie Sprinkle and Marc Stevens.

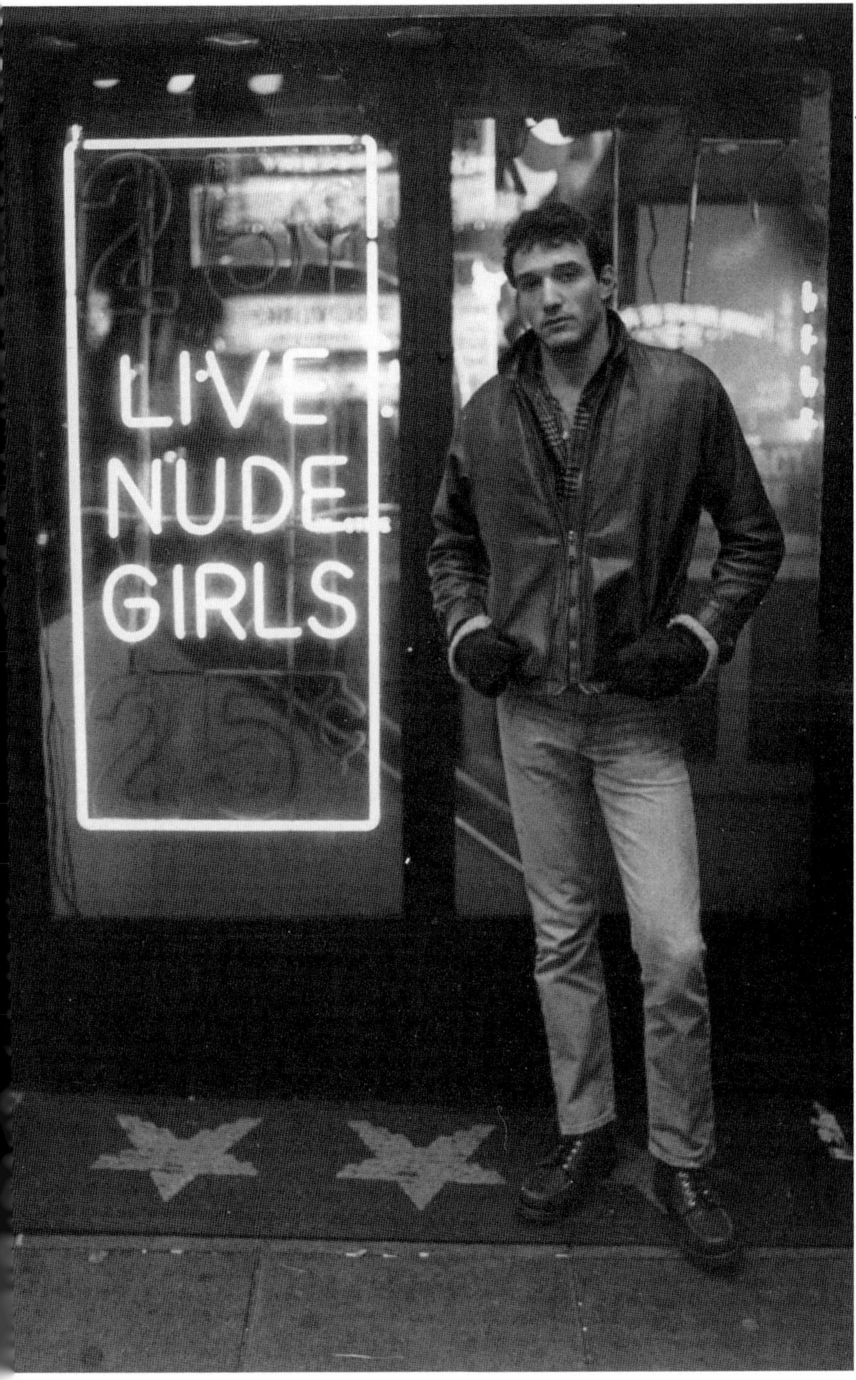
LIVE
NUDE
GIRLS

PRIDE OF THE YANKEES: The Great One, Al Goldstein, marshals instructions during twilight years of *Screw* and *Midnight Blue*.

SQUARE GUY: I always got the sense that Don Normal, right, always considered *me* the oddball.

A WORKING ACT: Former Hubert's attraction, Harold Smith, dispensing quarters at Playland, 1986.

BOSOM BUDDIES: "Mr. Burlesque," Bob Anthony, left, and B'way boxer Manny Rosen at the Melody B. in the late 70s.

FRIENDS IN LOW PLACES: Massey's proprietor, Bobby Sitton, visits pals at Oakwood Cemetery, Fort Worth, 1989.

of them doing methadone in the bathroom. I'm with the Bloods, the Crips, I'm the only white person, the oldest there. Handcuffed all the time. There's no diabetic food. Breakfast, lunch and dinner is the same—pieces of bread and jelly. Like a third world country, everything at Riker's was broken—the toilets, the sinks, the copying machines. Nothing to do but stare at space. It's filthy, there are cockroaches, everyone hates you, it's a fuckin' horror."

Some corrections officers asked Goldstein for his autograph. But the 20-year-old gangbangers had no idea who The Great Pornographer was. Even supporters within the NYPD were unable to sneak in pastrami sandwiches.

"I'm not some Mafia guy who can do time standing on my head. Theoretically, you're allowed to have visitors, but they wouldn't let me. I'm not talkin' theory, I'm talkin' truth. You can have *Penthouse*, *Playboy* and *Hustler*, but they wouldn't let me have *Screw*. They took *Newsweek*, *Time*, they took every magazine I had. They gave me only two—*Cigar Aficionado* just to aggravate me 'cause I can't smoke, and *Time Out*, the restaurant issue, since I wasn't allowed to eat. They're playing mind games, they're trying to break you." Lozinski got her revenge. In case there was a dearth of such creatures at Riker's, the guards got themselves one fat, angry, loudmouth New York Jew to aggravate. Not enjoying his stay, Goldstein was taken to the medical ward, where his *attitude* made him the ideal prisoner to torture. After seven hours waiting for permission to use a bathroom, Goldstein shit his pants. He refused to take a shower. "If I am to be in hell, I want to smell like hell," he told the guards. He began hallucinating, seeing double and hearing voices after being injected with God knows what.

"They performed surgery on me illegally. They put a catheter up my leg against my will in Riker's hospital. They stopped giving me my own diabetic medicine, they switched my anti-depressants to Zoloft, which I don't take. They injected insulin in my arm, which I don't take. It was Dr. Mengele. The corrections officer said I would leave in a pine box."

Watching CNN one night, an old man whose legs were amputated wheeled in and changed the channel over Goldstein's protest. "That was my one fight in prison and I yielded to a legless cripple," he says. "Let the cripple watch his nigger shows," Goldstein thought to himself, "I fucked Seka and Linda Lovelace. I'm sure the only girls this guy ever fucked were members of his own family."

Goldstein daydreamed of the steaks, lobsters and hookers he would ravish when he got out. He prayed for the first time in 42 years—since he was jailed in Cuba for photographing Raul Castro and told he would be executed as an American spy. Fahringer's legal assistant, Tricia Dubnow, came to Goldstein's rescue. "She saw me laying on the floor shaking, puking, crying. She would not leave without me."

Tricia got locked up herself for 25 hours trying to bail Al out.

His bail was accepted after nine days in Riker's. He still owes them 50 more days. His passport confiscated, he can't travel a radius of more than 20 miles from his Florida home or his New York apartment.

"They won, they broke my spirit," Al told *The New York Times*, stumbling out of Riker's nearly comatose. It was the first time he ever cried during an interview.

Jordan

"The first arrest embarrassed my son, who graduated Harvard Law School," Goldstein continues. "Now that he's Mr. Harvard he's so ashamed. Two weeks ago he called me at eight o'clock in the morning and, are you ready for this, here's the message he personally delivered to me: he said, 'Dad, the reason I didn't invite you to Harvard Law School's graduation wasn't because of Mom—but because *I* did not want you there. I cannot wait for the day I read your *New York Times* obituary.' I said, Fuck you, and I hung up. That was worse than all the other shit. I wake up in the middle of the night crying."

Before Harvard, Jordan Goldstein finished first in his class of 781 students at Georgetown University. The chart is framed on Goldstein's office wall. Al's son was offered graduate scholarships to NYU and Oxford. But Al Goldstein—a fat, former bed-wetting stutterer from Williamsburg, Brooklyn—*lived* for the day he could send his son to Harvard.

Al's own father was a small timid fellow who said "sir" to elevator operators. His last years were spent with a job in the *Screw* mailroom. Rather than live in fear and resignation, Goldstein became the opposite of his father. And now his son Jordan has become a conservative beacon of respectability. They now hate each other as only family members can.

Immediately after their fallout, Goldstein declared his son dead in the pages of *Screw*. This is how Goldstein vents his rage, the only way he knows how, the way he is designed. The ads Proud Papa Goldstein has been running of his son and ex-wife are clearly the rantings of a divine madman. The *piéce de résistance* of his career. Jordan is surrounded by an In Loving Memory wreath with his 1996 Georgetown Summa Cum Laude report card: "His academic achievements will not be forgotten by his grieving former father—who'd like to remind you that Jordan's Ivy League education cost him nearly $700,000." *Screw*'s subscription ads feature a mockup of Jordan in the gym: "Order...today, or you might end up turning into a spoiled, thieving, faggot Harvard boy..." Jordan's baby picture ("Wahhhh! I want my *Screw*!"). A "Who's Jordan's Dad?" contest to determine who knocked up Gina—with photos of possible impregnators Mike Tyson, Hitler, Bin Laden, Nixon, Arafat and blind Egyptian cleric Omar Abdel-Rahman. A full-page Reward offer appears each week, seeking Jordan Ari Goldstein's current whereabouts and number. A mockup photo of Gina blowing Jordan; Jordan blowing the President of Georgetown University; and one mock-up entitled "Nigger Lovin' Jews," showing Jordan and Gina copulating with Afro-Americans.

Gina may have once married The Great Pornographer, but Jordan didn't pick his dad.

"I was the greatest father, took him all over, filled him with love," says Goldstein, nearing tears. "I gave up my 25-year friendship with Hefner 'cause he would not let Jordan come to movie night at the [Playboy] Mansion. On the radio I've mentioned my son graduated Harvard Law School and how proud I was. I said, Jordan, if I were a surgeon, an entrepreneur, if I worked for Enron, you wouldn't worry about me being proud of you. I *kvell* at your success. Most people graduate college and law school owing hundreds of thousands of dollars. You have $300,000 in the bank. I spent $700,000 on Georgetown, on your tutoring, on Horace Mann School in the Bronx. Aren't I entitled to be proud? I went to Georgetown, I met the president, Father Donovan. We shared Cuban cigars. I always acted appropriate for the moment. I'm not Larry Flynt. It's in my will, Jordan can never enter my business, my world."

Goldstein kept *Screw* out of Jordan's reach when he was a small child. I once saw Al hide a wayward copy of *Playboy* on the banister at his 61st Street townhouse when Jordan was a toddler. Al shows a photo of himself, the picture of propriety with Harvard officials and Jordan. The education was paid for through a million tricks by prostitutes who advertise in *Screw*.

"I am so proud that he would travel the high road. The road I traveled, people are always surprised I could string together a sentence. We're in the porno world, we're never taken seriously. But his turning on me, wishing me dead… I thought Gina was responsible for that, that's why I called her a cunt."

A loud, interruptive voice cuts through Goldstein's campfire story. Enter Professor Irwin Cory. The geriatric comedian was a master of malapropism and double talk. An old Lefty, he joins the meeting, fuming about being rejected by the Communist Party in 1941. He curses "those *rats*" Burl Ives, Karl Malden and Elia Kazan, who squealed to the House Committee on Un-American Activities. "Indians never went to war at the command of captains or kings," intones Corey. "There isn't the word war in their vocabulary, nor the word warrior, or brave or chief or squaw, which is a vulgar expression. It means cunt. The Idaho Indians wanted that word taken out of any place that's named like Squaw Valley—change it to Cunt Valley."

"You know why I love you, Irwin?" says Goldstein. "You make me look sane. Will you come to court as a character witness?"

"Oh, yeah, I'll be there," says Corey, composing himself. "I'm a character that cannot be improved upon."

"Good," says Goldstein. "Your fucking courage to talk about the Vietnam War that got you banned from Johnny Carson and Letterman is why I will always love you."

Corey's voice rises to an abrasive scream, oblivious to all in the room, as he rails against the Catholic Church owning Yankee Stadium.

"Irwin Corey, you are a fuckin' hero," interrupts Al, trying to shut him up. "Will you absorb the praise and leave? You can't."

Goldstein heads to his private office while Corey lectures out of control to the *Screw* art department. "He's too disruptive, I can't handle him." There's only one other man as crazy as Corey—Al "Grandpa Munster" Lewis. "When they're together I run out of the room," says Al.

A man of the people, Goldstein's New York taxi cab hack license is posted on his office wall. He's kept it up to date since the 60s. Now and then, Goldstein claims, he hits the streets behind the wheel of a cab when he feels a need to stay down to earth. Plato's Retreat founder Larry Levinson ended up driving one, and so have a few male porn stars past their prime.

Though he claims he's just an old Jew who smokes cigars, he's got girls waiting in every city. Recent snapshots on the wall attest to this. He shares his primary residence in Florida with B-movie scream queen Linnea Quigley. An 11-foot hand sculpture in the backyard gives the finger to passing boats on the intracoastal waterway there. In Amsterdam, there's "Happy Hooker" Xaviera Hollander ("She's too old to do much but eat gefilte fish and take drugs with me."). In L.A., there's Katherine, an alumnus of "Hollywood Madam" Heidi Fleiss. He's dated her for six years, "though I know she's still gonna hook." Here at the office, he's having an affair with a 27-year-old knockout East Indian chick.

But the shocking news is that his number one bitch has become Jean-Marc—who suddenly appears through a swinging trap window in the wall by Goldstein's desk—right there in case of trouble. The Frenchman is Goldstein's bodyguard, flunkie... and Gal Friday. Jean-Marc's loyalty to Al has nothing to do with money. Al has proclaimed himself bisexual, getting it on with the Frenchman. He prefers him to some women.

"My last wife, Patty, got a million," says Goldstein. "I have no money. I'm living on Social Security." Al tried to play Pygmalion to fourth wife Patty, "the Irish cleaning lady." She kept right on working even after marriage. Al's limousine took her to cleaning jobs, though the limo cost $40 an hour while she was making $8.

Goldstein's now down to one elderly, part-time Jewish lady at the reception desk. Before he ever dreamed he would someday rely on Social Security, he employed four full-time secretaries. One for business appointments, one to take abusive dictation, and two to fill out daily mail-order catalog whims. He circled electronic *chotchkas* by the hundred—VCRs, CD players, model trains, calculators, solar-powered cigar lighters. His gold Mickey Mouse watch was studded with diamonds. A storage room at *Screw's* 14th Street headquarters was filled to capacity. His office still contains more gadgets than a gift shop. Only young girlfriends use the new $6,000 iPod at his desk. "I don't even know how to use a computer," he says. "I don't wanna learn at my age, my mind is filled."

Goldstein once published a magazine called *Gadget*, dedicated to his obsession with them (the party he was to throw at the *U.S.S. Intrepid* was for *Gadget's* anniversary). For his sudden obsession with cigars, he created the first publication solely devoted to the subject. In 1981, he flew five members of the *Screw* staff down to Havana with him. The Ugly American personified, Al inquired toward every Cuban what he could buy or take. For the return trip, he stuffed each staffer's suitcase with contraband cigars. After they squeaked through customs, Goldstein rifled through staffers' luggage, scattering clothes at the baggage claim as he pulled out his precious cigars.

His humidor filled to capacity, Goldstein stuffed cigars into every crevice of his wine cellar. One weekend a white fungus attacked all of his Havanas. In a panic, he rushed in two specialists from Dunhill's, wondering whether he should post an armed guard at the humidor. At editorial meetings, Goldstein discussed the logistics of sending us—his editorial staff—back to Cuba in a dinghy to smuggle another 10,000 Havanas. It would be cheaper than hiring mercenaries. Goldstein would await us at the Miami docks.

Goldstein has declared all of his noble ventures outside of *Screw*— *Gadget, Cigar, National Screw, Screw West, Sex Sense, Bitch, Gay, Death* and *Smut*—to be publishing failures. Only *Screw* has prospered, not having missed a week since 1968. Nearing 1,800 issues, Goldstein now believes the whole operation is in jeopardy of folding. He can't meet the payroll for the first time, can't even buy Deer Park for the water coolers, which are dried out like a desert. He's given up space in the new offices on 24th Street.

"It's my fault," admits Goldstein, "I travel too much. I deserve everything I got, I didn't manage the company. Right now I'm doing everything I can to keep from going out of business. If I go, nobody else is gonna be able to do it. It would just die."

There is no contingency plan if Al dies. One idea is to pretend he's alive, a Colonel Sanders with his cock out. Or sell his DNA like Ted Williams. Goldstein's good friend Bob Guccione might have been interested in saving *Screw*, but he has throat cancer and his own magazine is sinking. There was once talk of Larry Flynt buying it. "But even Larry doesn't have the insanity needed to helm *Screw*," says Goldstein. "You need someone who's filled with hatred. It's not driven by love."

Astro News in Brooklyn reports *Screw* is now selling only two copies each on 600 newsstands in New York. "That's not possible," says Goldstein. The circulation, at one time over 40,000, has now fallen to 5,000. Robert "DiBe" DiBernardo, the suave Gambino Family porn capo and Teamster liaison, was *Screw's* longtime protector. Back in the day, nobody could muscle Goldstein. Then DiBe disappeared in 1986. Ten years later Sammy "The Bull" Gravano disclosed in his biography, *Underboss*, that his crew aced DiBe by order of John Gotti.

Mayor Giuliani closed all the whorehouses, once the bulk of *Screw's* backpage ads. Free distribution of the *Village Voice* and *New York Press*, which began running the same ads once exclusive to *Screw*, cut deeply into circulation. And *Screw*, once piled high alongside the *New York Post* throughout the city, is now relegated to the back of the newsstand, due to Astro News.

But John Gotti has recently died in prison, and his son and his brother are in jail. "So now I'm making my move with a new distributor," Goldstein declares. "There's still the name *Screw* and the name Al Goldstein. I could go out of business quietly, or go fighting. So I made it clear I'm taking over distribution. This coming week is the first issue I take over. Another Family in Baltimore said they'd like to take over distribution. Astro News made it clear to me this can't happen, I'd be killed. I told Rick to go die. Rick left a message on my machine saying he'll destroy me and *Screw*. Rick basically wants to put *Screw* out of business and replace it with other papers he distributes."

The new distributor just paid 25 grand to take over distribution, and posted Al's $25,000 bail—an excellent show of faith. They got him a new apartment in Manhattan. The magazine will take on a glossy cover, rise to

$3.95, run a minimum 150 fuck photos per issue, and give a hefty new cut to each newsstand.

"If I'm found dead, beaten up, crippled or maimed," Goldstein tells the detective at his side, "you go to Rick at Astro News. He's behind it."

Having cops as friends doesn't hurt. In the 70s and 80s, Al's full-time bodyguard was a former NYPD vice squad cop who once busted hookers, as well as news dealers that sold *Screw* in the 60s. If some rookie tried to ticket Al's limo while idling in a No Parking zone, Flynn would shove his bearded face into their squad car and give them hell. Whenever the big debonair Irishman accompanied Al to 42nd Street, the Black streetwalkers had a field day. "Hey John Flynn, whatcha doin' John Flynn? You sho' is hot, John Flynn. Suck yo' dick, Officer Flynn?"

After years of faithful service to Milky Way Productions, the mother company of Goldstein's empire, John Flynn walked out of the limo to make a phone call. He left the keys inside. When he returned, the limo was gone. Goldstein gave him two weeks to find the car, or retire. The car was never found.

"If this experiment with *Screw* fails," says Goldstein, "I'm gonna try to kill myself in Pennsylvania. You don't wanna kill yourself in New York, L.A., Chicago or Florida. I have a girlfriend, she's 30, a great cocksucker. She went to a nuthouse in Pennsylvania. She gets a dental plan, health insurance and $800 a month support there.

"But I can't kill myself because Jordan owns a $1.2-million insurance policy on me. I got it as a gift to him when he graduated Georgetown. I don't want him to have the joy of cashing in the policy."

Al always said they'd have to fill up Yankee Stadium with suspects if he were killed. But he hasn't been. Not yet. He's outlived the anti-porn crusaders, the "evil puritans who loathe pleasure and want to deny it to everybody else," as he's described them.

"I'm not going to be everyone's fucking piece of shit, I'm not everyone's buttboy. I believe in the next year I'll either die in the Tombs or Riker's, where they said I'd leave in a pine box, or by an assassin's bullet."

To all the D.A.'s and judges, his family that turned against him, the Mafia threats and the system that killed Lenny Bruce, Al says: "I fuck you all. I dare you to try and stop me. You may kill me, but I won't go quietly."

And so The Great One ends his campfire discourse to enter the next room, where the new distributors await. Serious muscle from out of town. Men he does not want anyone at the office to meet. If it is to be his last weekend on earth, he will not go quietly.

CHAPTER SEVEN

PORNOGRAPHY HITS MAINSTREAM ON BROADWAY

A recent spate of mainstream studio releases delve into layers of the porn industry once deemed untouchable. The dumb and dumber-*Striptease* and *Showgirls* seemed targeted toward retarded folk, cheaply exploiting an enterprise known itself for exploitation. Both turkeys threatened to sabotage any intelligence in the realm of documenting the huge subject of sex.

The People Vs. Larry Flynt was notable mainly in that it portrayed Flynt as hero. Even the real Father of Pornography, Al Goldstein, proclaimed it superior to his own current documentary, *Screwed*. This year's *Boogie Nights*, however, is the cutest of this sudden Hollywood trend, an affectionate pat on the back to the 1970s generation of porno grind *auteurs*. But movies cannot match the cutting edge of theater.

Broadway raconteurs David Newman and Cy Coleman convene in Coleman's East Side townhouse a few weeks after *The Life* opened. Having just won some Drama Desk Awards, they are now anxious over upcoming Tony nominations—another hurdle in the marketing merry-go-round so crucial in keeping a multi-million dollar musical breathing. [*The Life* took Best Supporting Actor and Best Supporting Actress in a musical.]

"When I was first looking at theaters for this show," recalls Cy Coleman, "I said to the 42nd Street Authority: 'Let's make the whole street musical comedies. Put revivals in one or two theaters only, but make them all musical comedies.' I was charmed by these theaters. They smelled terrible, but you could see how beautiful they were.

"But the owners didn't like my idea. They wanted to diversify with a dance school, a children's center—*that* would bring people to 42nd Street. I said, 'If you're worried about getting a lot of people back, I have a great idea for you.' They asked, 'What is it?'

I said: 'Pornography.'"

The Life, on Broadway of all places, far surpasses the depth of any of the new crop of films paying historical homage to the sex industry (*Boogie Nights*, *The People Vs. Larry Flynt*, etc.). It's an all-singing, all-dancing look back at Times Square's street hookers and pimps. The heir to *Guys & Dolls*, 50 years later. So authentic are the hookers in the Cy Coleman-Ira Gasman-David Newman musical, at the Ethel Barrymore Theatre on 47th Street, that a former Times Square vice cop hangs out backstage each night, pining for his old beat. One expects to see a lineup of stagedoor johns soliciting the cast of streetwalkers. These girls could stop plenty of traffic by the Lincoln Tunnel. They bring back a fine lot of Times Square memories.

But isn't it too early for nostalgia?

"We didn't want it to be nostalgic at all, it's not the good old days," insist both authors.

Coleman purchased the fabled Steinway piano in his office when just a lad. The same 88's on which he composed the standards "Witchcraft," "Hey, Look Me Over," "If My Friends Could See Me Now," and "Big Spender." The hallowed chair opposite the piano has hosted "everybody's ass you can think of," says Newman. Theatrical flanks the likes of Bob Fosse, Jerome Robbins, Tony Bennett, Dorothy Fields, Liza and Mama Judy before her, the buttocks of Compton and/or Green.

"We're not endorsing bringing [pornography] back, no more than a play about Ivanhoe endorses the Crusades," Coleman maintains—a subject he must walk a tightrope on. "The reason we did the show was for the human story underneath about an environment that existed. All the theater owners were wary. But when the Shuberts realized this was a compelling story about people, we won over."

Gerald Shoenfeld, big boss of Broadway's eternally dominant Shubert Organization, sat among advisory boards like the 42nd Street Development Corporation that struggled exactly 20 years to "clean up" Times Square. And at the very moment in which 42nd Street received its baptismal clean slate—Disney's reopening of the once-doomed New Amsterdam—this $7-million musical on the golden age of pornography opened at the Ethel Barrymore, a *Shubert* theater.

"Remember that Cole Porter song, 'Please Don't Monkey with Broadway'?" says author of the book, David Newman, breaking into song. "'*You can glor-if-y Fifth Av-e-nue, tear down the zoo, but please don't monkey with Broad-way.*'"

The Life, though unintended as such, is a ringing rebuke to Disney.

"It feels like a theme park in Cincinnati," says Coleman of the 42nd Street area, "not even in New York."

Two Cy Coleman hits, *Sweet Charity* and *The Will Rogers Follies* originally played The Palace Theatre, once vaudeville's Mount Olympus. *Charity* opened The Palace's first renovation in 1966. "I hate it," Coleman says of the garish skyscraper recently forced upon its roof. "It was an institution, they should have kept the grand marquee on the corner. If you're gonna dress up Broadway, dress it up the dressiest way you can."

I suggest that *The Life* picks up Times Square 50 years after *Guys & Dolls*. The creators do not take this as an insult. The show depicts a credible representation of the culture that once gripped Times Square like Pottersville in *It's A Wonderful Life*. Dancing three-card monte sharks and pimps straddle 8th Avenue shoeshine stands waving racing forms, bemoaning the cops. Gospel-spouting evangelists replace the Salvation Army missionaries of Damon Runyon's day. This is Broadway with balls, and you wonder just who the audience is supposed to be. An elderly couple bolted last Tuesday, during "Don't Take Much," Tony-winning Chuck Cooper's show-stopper on pimp sorcery:

> *Ain't no trick to turn a hick into a hooker*
> *Not with all the hocus pocus that I know*
> *Ain't no trick to turn a hick into a hooker*
> *Ain't no thing that I ain't done befo'*
>
> *Don't take much to turn a girl into a woman*
> *Don't take much to set the devil in her free*
> *All it takes is a cold-blooded, sweet-talking, jive-ass,*
>   *mother-fuckin' son-of-a-bitch*
> *Like me*
> (Ira Gasman, lyrics; Cy Coleman, music)

"Those kind of walkouts remind me of when we did *Little Me* years ago." recalls Coleman. "Neil Simon was standing in the back. This guy storms out in the middle of the first act, and he looked at Neil Simon and says, 'This is the worst thing I've seen since *My Fair Lady*.'"

Throughout the 1970s, some 1,200 streetwalkers took up posts along 8th Avenue. An army of black pimps were headquartered at the Westerly, a high rise on 54th Street that stared down upon the Midtown North police precinct.

It was lyricist Ira Gasman who conceived of them *all-singing, all-dancing*. He wandered the neighborhood during those times, infatuated with the street, bearing witness to hooker-pimp psychodramas. "He had this revelatory moment and realized these people had the same kind of lives that he or anybody did," Newman explains. "They just happened to make their living in a tawdry profession. He got interested out of sympathy and identification."

"I think there was an element of admiration for the pimps, the way they dressed," adds Coleman.

"At an earlier stage, this show took place in the mid-'70s," Newman contends. "Then we were confronted with the AIDS problem. You can't do it without AIDS because the audience will think all these people are engaging in unsafe sex, without knowing what's around the corner. On the other hand, you can't do it post-AIDS, because then it's a bummer, you think these characters are irresponsible, they're spreading diseases. So we picked this date—1980—the very year when people were saying, 'There's something going around, but we don't know what it is.' So when [one of the hookers] says she ain't feelin' right, I don't know what it is, it ain't V.D. or no kinda clap, the audience knows, but *she* doesn't."

The Life recognized each prototypical maiden from Times Square's former shantytown of sex:

"That was very carefully considered," says Newman of the ladies. "We see the 300-pound, frizzy-haired Black mama, who perhaps chose the life over domestic work; the corn-fed, blue-eyed cheerleader from the mythical 'Minnesota Strip,' who arrived by Greyhound [played with wicked innocence by Bellamy Young]." In 1980s Times Square, it was disgraced Covenant House priest, Father Bruce Ritter, who falsely perpetuated the "Minnesota Strip" for fundraising purposes.

"I'd been around Times Square, put my share of quarters in peep shows," says Newman, who carried a token from Show World on opening night as a good luck charm. "We were extremely concerned with the distinctive individual types that are on that stage. Some of them are incredibly hot-looking, others are... well, every man has different tastes. There's a chubby white girl, a Puerto Rican girl who's not a raving beauty."

"Once at Christmas," reveals Coleman, "I was with a good friend, a woman. We'd never seen a live sex show so we went to Show World. And that was it, *my* whole experience."

One character in *The Life* was inspired by Silky, a 1970s pimp who received notoriety for the coffee-table book, *Gentleman of Leisure*. Silky's career was cut short after a promotional appearance on *The Mike Douglas Show*, where he announced he made "more money than the president of the United States." A brace of IRS agents promptly appeared at his crib, resulting in a lengthy prison stretch. Like many in his ranks, Silky dreamed of cleaning his act up and entering the record biz, according to Newman, who knew him from Elaine's Restaurant.

"His real name was Porky, but he changed his name to Silky for the book. He loved to hang around writers, and writers love to hang around gangsters, so there's always been that symbiotic relationship. This was an important piece of source material when I came into this project. *Gentleman of Leisure* got passed around between the costume guy, the hair guy and the director, and we have a character in the show named Silky."

Many players from the Pimp Liberation days of *Superfly* were shot, overdosed, imprisoned or ended up with shoe-shine stands. Few women fared better. Unlike the grand tradition of shows about hookers or strippers, from *Gypsy* to *Irma La Douce*, *The Life* is not sanitized. Certainly *The Life* couldn't have appeared on Broadway 20 years ago, when its subject matter pulsated right outside the theater. Even *Gypsy* didn't emerge until two decades after Mayor La Guardia shut down Minsky's Burlesque in Times Square.

"*Sweet Charity* was about hookers in Italy," says Coleman, of his mid-60s musical on the oldest profession. "But hookers on a street in Rome, standing in the park yelling out insults to guys walking by was quite different than hookers in New York."

The first reading in the 10-year odyssey to develop *The Life* occurred in front of an audience at the New Victory on 42nd Street. Before the book existed, Cy Coleman and Ira Gasman pushed their score, releasing a "concept album" long before the show opened.

"My idea was to bring it back to the old days when we used to introduce show songs beforehand," says Coleman. "When I was writing in the '60s, people were anxiously waiting to hear what the new songs of a show were. Now the record companies are not so anxious to give you their top stars for show material. So I put together a bunch of pop singles from *The Life* to make them familiar before the show came out."

Never before have Broadway songwriters had to work so hard at salesmanship. When Coleman wrote *Sweet Charity*, Streisand, Peggy Lee and Tony Bennett recorded pop singles prior to the show. "It was the greatest merchandising-marketing thing you could have, and it cost you zip." Traditionally, Broadway songwriters got their songs over this way. "The reason they'd say it's a tuneful score is because they heard it before. That old line about walking into the theater whistling the tunes, as opposed to walking out."

The Life concept album tempered the savagery of the songs—which evolved to a full boil by the time they reached the cast album. Coleman engaged Lou Rawls, Liza Minnelli, Bobby Short and finessed George Burns' very last performance, at age 100. Coleman himself, who sings as good as say, Fred Astaire, topped them all. He sings "A Lovely Day to Be Out of Jail," the album's most charming and simple track.

Though no Lincoln Tunnel whore likely ever sang "A Lovely Day To Be Out of Jail," upon release, such sentiment comes off naturally in the context of a Broadway show. The song "My Body" could be a pro-choice song, but appears as a hooker's pride anthem.

From Iceberg Slim's literary *oeuvre* came the concept of "The Hooker's Ball." Pimps toasted glasses and pitted their whore's talents against each other. It was an actual yearly event from a bygone civilization of vice ("*Though there is no Mother Goose, there really is a hooker's ball*").

"The Oldest Profession," the night's show-stopper, presents Best

Supporting Actress Lillias White as Sonja, a weary black hooker. After the girls figure she's turned 15,000 tricks according to a calculator, she rubs her swollen feet and settles her sore ass upon the barstool. The song only alludes to that most tired of her assets (never directly mentioning her puss, which would have lost the show some financing).

> *I'm gettin' too old for the oldest profession*
> *I'm gettin' too tired and too slow*
> *I'm gettin' too old for the half-hour session*
> *I'm gettin' too old for a pro*
> *I'm gettin' too old for to climb all those stairs, now*
> *A half-dozen times every night*
> *I'm gettin' too old for to take 'em in pairs, now*
> *Or to take off my clothes in the light*
> (Ira Gasman, lyrics; Cy Coleman, music)

Prototype bars for *The Life* included the former lowlife paradise Terminal Bar on 8th Avenue, and defunct strippers' hangout Bernard's, across from the old Melody Burlesk, which Newman once visited with porn actor Jaime Gillis. The bartender in *The Life*, who performs "The Hooker's Ball" was a composite of the dapper valets of Basie, Ellington and Lucky Millender, sidekicks whose loyalty kept them at their bandleaders' sides for decades. "Those guys would finally end up running a bar. There's a certain sweetness and elegance about our bartender, from a different era," says Newman of the role. "He's a comforting character for the audience, a hoofer from an earlier Broadway."

David Newman's legend began during the Kennedy era as an *Esquire* editor, where he invented the Dubious Achievements Awards. He was co-librettist of the 1967 Broadway gem, *It's A Bird, It's A Plane, It's Superman*—as well as co-screenwriter of *Bonnie & Clyde* and the three *Superman* movies. He recalls the 42nd Street of his childhood, a honky-tonk highway of Playlands, Hubert's Museum, Grant's hot dogs and the Laffmovie Theater, which ran endless Three Stooges, Leon Errol and Laurel & Hardy shorts before TV existed. (Coleman wisely suggests they revive this exact same bill at some comedy club in Times Square.) In the 60s, Newman took his son Nathan to see double-feature westerns at the Selwyn. Newman also had a serendipitous run-in with *Glen or Glenda* at the Rialto, then billed as *I Changed My Sex*, starring Bela Lugosi. "I called [former partner] Robert Benton at *Esquire* and said I'm not coming back to work this afternoon. Invent a reason to come over here, I'll be in row five. We called our wives and said, 'Get baby sitters, meet us at six o'clock, you gotta see this fuckin' movie.'" Newman saw *Glen or Glenda* three times that day, writing perhaps the first-ever piece on Ed Wood for *Film Comment*. Such was the wonder of 42nd Street.

Coleman avoids seeing high school productions of his shows, but was amazed to hear one was done of *City of Angels*. "Somebody reliable told me they did a terrific job, all that difficult scat-singing that I wrote down. Kids will go for the challenges."

Will *The Life* be done by a high school someday?

"College, yes," says Coleman. "They'd have to be a very enlightened high school. It depends upon the popularity of the show. *West Side Story* and *Porgy And Bess* took a lot of flak about gangs or drugs. Now they're classics. When you're around long enough, people pick them up as classics, then they start to deal with them as a piece of art."

—*1997*

CHAPTER EIGHT

AN ICEBERG SLIM APPRECIATION

Years after covering Times Square, I belatedly discovered writers of generations past who walked the same beat—Damon Runyon, A.J. Liebling, Joseph Mitchell—and Iceberg Slim, from Chicago.

A mere 20 years ago, in the 70s, the "canon" of Negro Lit—Black American novelists in print—was preposterously thin, scattered and barely represented at mainstream bookstores. A handful of chosen authors received literary knighthood, but no matter how you sliced it, James Baldwin's lofty intellect landed squarely in the liberal white establishment. One-hit wonders, like Ralph Ellison's 1952 *Invisible Man*, or Claude Brown's 1964 bestseller, *Manchild in the Promised Land*, were grounded in the Queen's English—as was the great Richard Wright before them, whose lean, mean prose hammered home the Negro experience to generations of college Caucasians.

Iceberg Slim burst forth in 1969 as a savagely gifted storyteller, whose paperback novels sold in unprecedented numbers in the ghettos. Iceberg Slim was the nom-de-pimp of Robert Beck, whose seven books sold six million copies by the time he died in 1992, at age 73. Beck briefly graced Tuskegee Institute's 1930s college rolls at the same time as did Ralph Ellison. Beck dropped out, having chosen his calling—for which Tuskegee offered no degree. Years later, had it come to a streetfight of words, Iceberg's "masterworks of pimp profanity" could have cut down Ellison's milquetoast prose in a Harlem minute.

He wrote flagrantly in the pre-Ebonics lingo of Chicago's South Side—which even today repels the upwardly mobile Black middle class. Iceberg's books contain glossaries of underworld Negro slang that went out with minstrel shows and burnt cork blackface. The *Norton Anthology of Black American Literature*—newly christened by Black Harvard professors proclaiming a breakthrough, state-of-the-art "canon"—doesn't even mention his name in its vast index.

Like the painter Grandma Moses, Iceberg Slim was reborn an artist after age 40. His third, and harshest, prison sentence—10 months in steel solitary at the Cook County House of Corrections—finally crushed the pimp right out of him. Vilifying past predatory values, he exorcised his demons into folklore, leaving a seven-book legacy. *Pimp: The Story of My Life*, contained bookend warnings against the life. But Iceberg's masterpiece only bolstered pimp liberation amidst the blaxploitation movie craze. In Times Square, for instance, a hundred fur-coated Superflys lorded over a thousand streetwalkers, taking renegade control of 8th Avenue. For them, *Pimp* declassified the sorcery of whore control, became a textbook for wannabe's and lent ethnic pride to the hideous profession.

Pimp still holds as perhaps the greatest chronicle ever written on male-female relations. In the flush of literary success, white feminist-journalist types sought out interviews like intellectual groupies. Pimp philosophy, Iceberg believed, might be adapted to mainstream relationships. "My theory is that some quantum of pimp in every man would perhaps enhance his approach to women," he told the *Washington Post*. "Because I think it's a truism that women gravitate to a man who can at least flash transient evidence of heelism... Women are prone to masochism, anyway. I think if you are able to manufacture a bit of 'heelism' in your nature and give them a sense of insecurity as to whether some voluptuous rival might come along and steal you, then you are a treasured jewel."

The thrill, Iceberg told the *L.A. Free Press*, came during youth, where he described "a vacuum that is filled by the joy of learning the intricacies of being a pimp... For really, what is the bedrock of all male aspiration, if it isn't cunt and money? Now here the pimp, what has he got? All kinds of beautiful girls, who bring him cunt and money. Kiss and suck and love him... on the surface, of course, because beneath, they really pray for his ruin."

An underlying trait common to career pimps, Iceberg found, was a hatred of mama. "I've known several dozen, in fact, that were dumped into trash bins when they were... only four or five days old."

Pimping was a Black man's hustle. Iceberg claimed he never saw a white player in his league. Whites were rare, he explained, "because there's so many other areas of chicanery, which are much more lucrative, that are open to white fellows." Iceberg referred to white women, in the historical sense, of course, as "alabaster supercunts."

Black pimps of yore (denied entry into the corporate death culture they enjoy today) chose to use their superior intellect to enslave women, avoiding the sucker's workaday world. But controlling 10 women at a time could really fray a fellow's nerves. One must summon endless schemes and deceptions to stay one step ahead of his treacherous charges: "A pimp is happy when his whores giggle," Iceberg wrote. "He knows they are still asleep."

One wrong turn, and Candy Man Dan might "blow whoreless."

Iceberg told the *Washington Post* he retired from the life at age 42 "because I was old. I did not want to be teased, tormented and brutalized by young whores." Girls raised on TV, brainwashed by its tease of material wealth, could no longer fall for the cheap glamour once utilized by Iceberg's generation of pimps. (In those days, a pimp could tack upon his hotel wall yard rolls of satin from the fabric store, and dazzle the bitches.)

His second novel, *Trick Baby*, abounded with the preposterous racial torments that Blacks and whites alike once rained upon the poor mulatto or octoroon. Any such person, it was once assumed in the ghetto, must surely be the offspring of a Black prostitute and a white trick—thus the title *Trick Baby*. (Talk about your snap judgments!)

Iceberg Slim's second novel was the story of his prison mate, Chicago con man Johnny O'Brien, of Irish-African blood—known as "White Folks" to his friends, "Trick Baby" to his enemies. Looking like the twin of Errol Flynn, Folks could have entered white society, but spent his early career on Chicago's South Side, preferring to flimflam his own people.

Folks fell insanely in love with a white blueblooded "Goddess." In perhaps the most wrenching revelation ever written in the annals of race relations, he blurts out his darkest secret—that he is actually a "coon."

"Mrs. Costain, you have a bona-fide bastard nigger baby in your sacrosanct guts," he reveals. White Folks suffered an alcoholic nervous breakdown over his Goddess breakup. After his childhood mentor, master con man Blue Howard, dies, Folks leaves his side of the tracks to practice con in the high-finance white world. Iceberg continues the story of *Trick Baby* in his novel, *Long White Con*.

Iceberg's prose did indeed grow loftier as his success continued. One of the journalistic sketches collected in *The Naked Soul of Iceberg Slim*, shows him humbled before the Black Panthers: "Nigger, you kicked black women in the ass for bread. How many you got now?" comes a young Panther. Rather than chop him down with his "still-remembered masterworks of pimp profanity," Iceberg admits to himself that the Panthers are "superior to that older generation of cowards, of which I am part." He leaves with "genuine tears rolling down my joyous old nigger cheeks."

Holloway House, the independent Black publishing group in Los Angeles, represents an alternative Black universe in paperback. Mysteries, Westerns, romances, crime sagas, biographies. Holloway spokesman Mitchell Neal says *Pimp* has sold 2 1/2 million copies to date. Neal brazenly states *no* books by Black authors were available during the 1960s—not only dismissing Black establishment writers of the era, but poets (Leroi Jones), playwrights (Ed Bullins, Melvin Van Peebles), show-biz bios (Sammy Davis' *Yes I Can!*, Pigmeat Markham's *Here Come Da Judge!*) and numerous political manifestos. But Iceberg Slim has remained Holloway's flagship writer since 1969, followed by the *oeuvre* of Donald Goines (16 titles). A half-dozen pimp memoirs, for instance, followed on the heels of *Pimp*—whose author steadfastly remains America's true pimp-laureate.

After Iceberg Slim became the American ghetto's best-selling author, he released a masterful performance album of poetry called *Reflections* in the early '70s. The timbre and meter of his voice is so hypnotic, it takes no stretch of the imagination to see how he sweet-talked hundreds of wavering females into the world's oldest profession. Such a demonstration, in fact, is reenacted for your listening pleasure on the opening vignette, "The Fall."

We can only speculate that Iceberg's literary education in prison included the discovery of poet Robert W. Service, whose meter he emulated. Service wrote doggerel epics at the turn of the century, like "The Cremation of Sam McGee." As Service wrote of what he knew—the Klondike and the Gold Rush—so did Iceberg write what he knew, using the form made popular by Service.

At the age of 55, with four young children, he said, "Now my ambition is to be as good a father as I was a pimp." Anxious to feed those four hungry beaks, as well as cushion their future, the middle-aged dad wrote, gave lectures and stayed square. It was tough adjusting from Big Daddy to just plain daddy. At first, his infant daughters were like "little whores," he said. He had a morbid fear of being kissed by them, and would only pick up his kids with their backs toward him. Through grit and determination, and the aid of his new wife, Iceberg eventually fit in—comfortably niched in Los Angeles halfway between Ward and Eldridge Cleaver.

—1995

CHAPTER NINE

KELLIE EVERTS

I attended Mass with Kellie Everts, the paradoxical Williamsburg, Brooklyn-based "stripper for God." We went to her local parish, the Church of Annunciation. Bowed down at the pew, her enormous breasts straining against a proper yellow blouse, her buttocks arched heavenward, I watched her lips recite the gospel, word for word with Father Michael at the pulpit, her eyes closed. Clerestory windows of stained glass rose up to the peak of this cathedral, resplendent with Christ statuary and the wealth of the Catholic Church.

A "woman of big breasts," as Kellie referred to herself, can bring thousands to the Lord. Kellie can personally account for hundreds of conversions she has garnered for the church, mostly during nude sermons on burlesque stages, after her strip, in which she proselytizes the word of Jesus until they run her off. More than a few strip joints have blacklisted her. Here in church, however, sex and religion seemed a distant, but potent, combination—who could possibly climax better than someone with deep religious convictions?

But Kellie Everts, unfortunately, has remained celibate for the past seven years. "I made a solemn vow with the Blessed Virgin in 1978 to stay celibate. Sex is a sin. It would be tough now to have sex. Sometimes I have a very slight desire, but I channel it into different things. The first secret of celibacy is not to dwell on the thought or concept of sex. If you do, chemicals start moving in your body. The first year was the hardest."

Celibacy is the second paradox of Kellie Everts. Stripping is the first, the profession from which she earned international fame from in the 1970s, the reason she is a pariah at the Catholic Church, to which her heart and soul belong. This is her cross to bear—she feels God put her here to go among the lost souls of red-light districts, where clergy dare not roam. She is the only evangelist/stripper known, and the new set of sizzling spread shots she posed for *Adam*, *Fox*, and a half-dozen tit mags, like *Big Boobs*, will not exactly cause men's peckers to fall off from under-abuse. She'll list a hundred ways to jusify her cause, but not one solid answer:

"The men who see my spreads—*they're* not celibate. I'd rather be a nun. I applied to the Transfiguration Monastery Convent in Windsor, New York; they turned me down. They wouldn't give me a chance. They read about me in the paper. I can't make it in the legit world because I'm too well-known. I don't consider stripping or posing a sin, but I'll admit it's not good either. If I had to have sex for money, for a living, it would be less sinful. But if I do it to get my rocks off, for pleasure, that is *lust*. I would be feeding my lust, my sensuality, being a glutton. Like gorging out on junk food."

Kellie always felt guilty after sex, she says, because of her Catholic upbringing. She was strongly indoctrinated by nuns as a child, something she never forgot after getting laid.

"Sex was my only bad habit. I needed it as a release, otherwise I'd have gone crazy, because of all the aggravation I put up with saving souls, serving God and helping people. It took years of discipline to quit, but the craving goes away."

Only one object in this world could break Kellie Everts from her sacred vow of celibacy: "Tom Selleck. I used to be in love with him." Her self-published book, *Knowing and Loving Tom Selleck*, is the only manuscript among the dozen that Kellie wrote and sells mail-order that doesn't deal solely with mystical theology. I asked whether she ever worked with the TV star.

"I wish. He knows I'm celibate, but I would have slept with him if he tried to persuade me. The reason God never allowed me to meet him was because if he had tried to make love to me, I would have given in. I would have broken my vow of all those years of celibacy, I would have felt suicidal, like a degenerate; I'd probably impose some sort of penance on myself. The first time I saw Tom Selleck on TV I had a climax in my sleep that night. I was so ashamed, I promised God I would never look at him again. If I turned on the TV, I made sure it wasn't Channel 2; if I saw him on the newsstand, I quickly looked away."

In January 1974, Tom Selleck actually called for Kellie when she was stripping at the Hubba Hubba Club in Hawaii. She'd gone to the *Magnum P.I.* casting director to sign on as an extra for the show. She didn't get a part, but he invited her to the set where they bullshitted a while.

"By the time I finally met him, I was in a more spiritual state of mind, but before then I would have gone insane with desire where I'd have no control. Because he's so hairy. I asked him to unbutton his shirt. I was never into hair till I met him. His father and girlfriend were there. If I could have sex with him, my human nature would probably feel happy, but my higher nature would condemn me. I would waver between depression and joy—'Oh, boy, I screwed Tom Selleck, the man I love!' But my higher self would say, '*You pig.*'"

"I asked God, and He told me that the men who look at these are *already* lustful, and that I'm not recruiting new people." Kellie Everts justified her new set of nude color slides, sitting at Kellog's Diner in Williamsburg, Brooklyn. "God put me where I am needed the most. No matter what the world thinks to the contrary, I am here to save people through pornography and nudity. I am the only minister He sent into this field."

Kellie did say this with an ironic smile, but her sincerity was pure. "How do you like these for boob shots?" she asked, unveiling a pair of breathtaking 46D's, being sent to *Gent*. *Velvet*, *Big Boobs*, *Adam*, *Fox*, *High Society* and *Leg Show* have run, or will soon run, new Kellie Everts spreads. *Max* ("Where the Double D-Cup Runneth Over") will be making Kellie their mascot cover girl. "I didn't know my asshole was showing here," she said of one lollapalooza. More than a third of Kellie's following are tit fans. She revealed some jealousy held for one of her competitors: "If I only had Candy Samples' size boobs, I could market them so much better than her."

Five new churches have opened in Kellie's part of Williamsburg since she came here spreading her "divine light." This has been her turf since 1972. Kellie began her ministry among the poor Puerto Ricans, while supporting her work by headlining on the burlesque circuit. "I was minister and social worker, I had all the teenagers that I used to pick up from the streets. I started a youth center in my house. I was trying to teach them the Bible, but I found out they couldn't read. 18 years old, couldn't read. So I learned this was a different culture. I tried to branch out with Italians and Blacks, but they didn't need me. They have tighter family structures, they were already culturally indoctrinated. The crying need came from the Puerto Ricans. They have a lotta kids, and usually no fathers—the mothers might have several children, all with different fathers.

"Basically, people who are desperate will take anything you give them. They liked the idea that somebody cared and let them come to their house. I gave dancing lessons, took them on trips, we had rap sessions together. I was their mother superior, they were the disciples. One of my groups was a gang called the Vipers."

Kellie did this for four years, quitting in 1977 after she felt "burned out." Being savior to Brooklyn's Puerto Rican welfare kids took a toll. She never received donations. "My neighborhood was and is 90 percent welfare, even poorer than welfare." What further hampered Kellie's credibility as a clergywoman, along with stripping, was her hot romance with the skinny 17-year-old leader of the Vipers. (Certainly the most blasphemous union since evangelical icon Aimee Semple McPherson shacked up with the young and studly Milton Berle.) The Vipers were a teen biker gang, except they couldn't afford Harleys or even Yamahas, so they did their shootings on hot-rod bicycles. She thought Chinito was beautiful, even the way he picked his teeth with his knife. Photographer Jean-Paul Goude, with an eye toward emerging *spic chic*, did a famous photo spread of Kellie and the gang for *Esquire*, then for *Playboy*. The evangelist showed Goude a photo of Chinito's 10-inch *chorizo* at whopping full-mast, asking, "Isn't he cute?"

Stripping, she said, was no big deal; it went undiscussed at her Bible meetings. Any kid who acted "lustful" or disrespectful was booted out. When Chinito was present, there was no trouble. But once, Kellie returned from a vacation to find her apartment ransacked, desecrated with scumbags, all her belongings stolen. She suspected shithead gang members who had been ejected. On another occasion, when the owner of a local diner offered a nearby storefront as her youth center headquarters, the local Italian hierarchy threatened to bust up the man's diner. They didn't want Puerto Rican gangs hanging out in the neighborhood.

"The gang leader was my boyfriend for two years. In fact, I was thinking of marrying him. But that wasn't feasible because of age, cultural difference, intelligence. You can't have a person who was like a son; marriage partners have to have something in common mentally."

Kellie yearns for friendships with clergymen and nuns. When I accompany her back to the rectory of the Church of Annunciation after Mass, she lusts after the priest's intellectual attention. Having self-published eight books on mystical theology ($10 a pop, mail order), Kellie has been waiting to engage Father Michael's opinions on them. She believes 90 percent of all priests are homosexually inclined. If I wasn't with her, she claimed, this young priest wouldn't have given Kellie five minutes of his time. For subconscious hormonal reasons, however, he was willing to spend a half-hour with us.

In the rectory, Father Michael said he's read three of the manuscripts she presented to him. He took a deep breath, closed his eyes, threw his head back and searched for an opinion: "I first became familiar with the whole thing several years ago. There was an article on Kellie in the Sunday magazine section of the *Philadelphia Inquirer*. Initially, I didn't know this was the same person in church, but by the time she gave me the manuscripts, I put things together. It is quite an extraordinary juxtaposition there. I wanted to hear what she had to say, so I read the manuscripts."

The priest hemmed and hawed a bit more while Kellie Everts, the stripper for God, grew impatient for his views. "It's an impossible thing for a human being," said Father Michael, "to evaluate another human being's relationship with God... and how they act according to their conscience or what they see. That's not to say there are no objective norms. But only God is qualified to judge this. Therefore, I myself stay out of His territory in this matter."

Thus, we both heard perhaps the most liberal analysis possible from a clergyman concerning the paradox of Kellie Everts. Still, he withheld an opinion on her books. "If it were put to me, I would say, on the surface, these things [stripping and evangelism] are not compatible... There is a fundamental conflict here—the nature of the two professions. Her theological writing is God-centered. But the other, by nature, is not pointed toward God, though it's being diverted that way. It's a question of what we call an 'occasion of sin.' If someone is attracted to some particular sin of the flesh, then I wouldn't play from that attraction, to have it pointed at them, then say, 'Wait a minute, now look at God!'"

Kellie can't settle on a definitive answer. "It's like there's a power greater than me that told me stripping is what I had to do, whether I want to or not," she told the priest. "Nobody believes or understands me, but this is my cross."

Father Michael cites the example of another priest, Father Depaul, who takes flak for conducting his ministry around street hookers and combat zones. "Yet he's not personally involved in it himself—he doesn't manage a theater."

Kellie attends Mass twice a day and is sometimes the only worshipper present for the second one. They take her for granted in Williamsburg. She's not sure about going back on the strip-stage circuit. She received death threats after she'd been on the local news in San Francisco, causing a cancellation at the Mitchell Brothers theater. She often donates part of her hefty burlesque salary to local church funds, "for Masses for the Souls in Purgatory." (One of her books, *The Deliverance of Errol Flynn From Purgatory*, is a "true story" describing Kellie's five-month rescue operation and conversations with the dead movie star, culminating in his deliverance.)

What Kellie desired now was a sex magazine editorship. "I could pose for pictures every week. I'd run around, scouting for models. I can appreciate beautiful women from an artistic point of view, but not to have sex with them."

The Stripper for God believes other starlets degrade themselves in porn or lesbianism. Kellie has never yet involved herself in hardcore porn, other than splaying tits, ass and twat as the Lord created it. She was the first female body builder in the United States, her six-page spread in *Esquire* introducing the concept. After the layout appeared, Honeysuckle Divine, then *Screw*'s own outrageous stringer, latched onto Kellie. In the early '70s, Honeysuckle was billed on Times Square burlesque marquees as "The Dirtiest Girl On Earth." No one had a clue that she was really a Jekyll/Hyde case. A nun who left the convent like a werewolf when the moon was full. Finally ousted from the church, she pined to return to the convent. Honeysuckle's desire to return to God, juxtaposed with her arresting porn career, had sent her careening into a loony bin. Kellie Everts, a kindred spirit, performed exorcisms on Honeysuckle, ridding pornography demons from her soul. Honeysuckle returned to holy communion, studying the sacraments and living incognito in the straight world.

And so, where priests and nuns dare not roam, Kellie Everts fishes her hooters out in the name of God. One soul is a lot to save, but few souls take her seriously. Though she incorporated her own School of Sainthood in Brooklyn and first introduced the sport of female bodybuilding, she has credibility problems. Not one feminist will stand beside her when she crusades for rights of female sex workers, or espouses female superiority. The Catholic Church will honor no serious theologist who splays gorilla crotch. Her mail-order catalogs feature evangelical polemics like *The Holy Trinity Within the Mortal Soul*. Sold side-by-side with tracts like "My Horny Proctologist" and "If You Love Me, Eat My Shit." This is her cross to bear.

—1985

CHAPTER TEN

WRITE & FIGHT

"**L**ook, I'm the guy who wrote *Whomping the Wasps*, I realize that. Anything happens to me, that's what I'm remembered for," says Pete LeSand, downing another beer. Sadly, no one knew of his only published novel, released by the University of Cleveland Press in a limited-run militant-writers series. Pete's lopsided, pockmarked head, the result of a clumsy forceps delivery, smiled goofily from the dust jacket 20 years earlier. That he insists this book was his crowning achievement, and possibly his swan song, is a rare admission that he hasn't yet followed up with another. Or made a big name for himself in journalism. Not that the book didn't ring with some bizarre rhythm of metaphorical, violent poetry. Pete's life is charged with political and literary fury, as well as brawling romance and street fighting.

We're out dancing with welfare mothers at the Holland Hotel on 42nd Street. "Strokin'" is on the juke, over and over, while Pete declares he is "the best white barroom dancer in New York." He gyrates soulfully, not a word spoken, with homeless Black women who come up to him—not me—at our barstools.

I am the Times Square beat reporter for the *New York Dirt*, Gotham's progressive daily in a four-paper town. Got me a little column squeezed between the harness-racing scores and the Earl Scheib car-refinish ads. Valuable space for strippers plugging Big Apple engagements.

So Pete, totally independent of me, lands a job at the *Dirt* features desk.

He's to hand in one story per week, for which he's paid $350 off the books. Stories on boxers, founders of maverick martial-arts academies, blue-collar factories in the boroughs. This is his first steady cash in years, so here we are celebrating.

"I know I'm being exploited by those pigs!" chimes Pete. "And *you're* being exploited, too!" he spits. "They've got you writing about these pathetic fallen women who pander to lost souls in burlesque theaters. Why give credibility to those no-talent broads in print?"

I like my job, thank you, but Pete wouldn't hear it. And he eats up his first weekly check like a starving vacuum cleaner.

Some welfare mom with frizzy copper hair taps his shoulder for another go-round on the dance floor. Pete soulfully obliges. Driven by a lusty curiosity, Pete has slept with a few of them. If you ask me, this is going a tad too far. But not so far as the time he admits to "making love" with a pre-op transsexual, which he followed home on Ninth Avenue. "Weirdest scene I ever saw," says Pete. "But you gotta be tough to survive a night with one of them and not get your throat cut," he says, like some jailyard boast.

The barkeep at the Holland adds a touch of magic on his shift. Every night at three a.m.. someone delivers a hot batch of White Castles, imported from Queens Boulevard, across the river. White Castle's 39-cent hamburgers are a true delicacy in Manhattan, where the chain never opened a franchise. This is an enigma I'll have to do a column on.

The welfare mothers wangle a few more beers out of us, before retiring to their reeking hotel SROs upstairs, that cost the city a scandalous $750 per week each. Their kids wander dazed before the hotel entrance. Pete dribbles a basketball with a few on the cracked sidewalk at 42nd and 9th, after we close the bar at four.

The next evening, as we make our way toward Jimmy Ray's Saloon on Eighth Avenue, who do we run into but none other than Elsa Kay, brunette porn starlet. Elsa is the scion of a noted academic family, her father being president of a large institution of higher learning. She too received a master's degree, in impressionist art, then promptly switched careers. Elsa never quite gained top billing to carry an X-rated flick by herself, but figures nicely as a second banana. So she moonlights, turning tricks in Little Italy and Harlem, by appointment only, with union officials and important men in the cement industry.

Elsa tells us she's just gotten back from a month working the Alaska pipeline, where it was very cold. But she cleaned up, what with Alaskan inflation, and the high wages earned by pipelayers looking to keep warm in the Klondike.

It may be presumptuous to say, but Elsa casts a sweet glance my way now and then. I always turn the other cheek, not wishing to mix work with hanky-panky. But tonight she's rolling in cold cash from Alaska, purse chock full of bills, and Pete gets this twinkle in his eye like he's struck the mother lode.

Elsa's blonde friend isn't too shabby either, a former Melody Burlesk headliner who went under the name Sophia Blaqulord. Of course, Sophia has returned to her Christian birth-certificate name, Margaret Letsky, and is one of the few to have left the stripping fame for a successful career, as a traveling cosmetics executive.

We're seated at a round table at Jimmy Ray's—the two dolls, Pete and I— with Pete ordering double shots. Never shy of opinions or lectures, Pete takes to the podium immediately. He's already finished an article on "ghettology," a defensive survival course for slum kids taught by some ex-con in Bed-Stuy. He's done another piece on "subway swordsmanship." But Pete's *pièce de résistance*, sure to revolutionize journalism, he predicts, is his first epic cover story for *New York Dirt*—to be called "Bennie the Benevolent."

Bennie is Pete's new best friend, the last of the great foremen on the Brooklyn shipyard docks. He reigns over a blood brotherhood of longshoremen, salt-of-the-earth working men, some of whom earn more money per hour than brain surgeons. Pete will chronicle Bennie's struggle to save his honorable profession from extinction in the modern world, as well as Bennie's romances and great acts of charity amongst the youth of Sheepshead Bay. Pete's story has plenty of local color, including the "Guidos"—handsome silverhaired men in their sixties who recline along Sheepshead Bay sipping wine in tank-top undershirts, sought out by 16-year-old Brooklyn girls in overdone makeup for sexual educations. A movie sale was inevitable for Bennie the Benevolent.

"You'll just have to meet him," Pete tells the girls. And I am invited to come out on Monday to watch him spar. For Bennie, I'm told, is also a man of huge arms and physique, who gave up a pro-boxing career for more altruistic callings. But he still spars with other heavyweights three times a week, as well as Pete, whom he has embraced beyond the workings of an article.

Emboldened by liquor, Pete extols the virtues of "real men" from the outer boroughs, men who live by a code of honor, who keep their word and defend their friends. Not like the cowardly, milquetoast sycophants who run publishing in Manhattan. Talentless little men, deadened to originality, whose only satisfaction comes from backstabbing, or leaving their footprints all over your story in a rewrite. Real men were no longer of Manhattan. Manhattan had been overtaken by investment bankers and Euro-trash, bored by the excess of their ill-begotten wealth as they aimlessly went club-hopping in their limos.

With this I can readily agree. Many an evening we'd mourned the city losing its soul. But the girls seem zoned out on Venus, somewhat. Pete's anger segues toward the loss of editing as a gentlemanly profession. *American Lense* had given him trouble on his combat-karate story:

"'Cut out the purple prose,' my editor says, 'too much purple prose.' I worked two months on that story. I told him, 'I can kill you and make it last for 18 minutes. I can bust your ribs, I can tear off an ear. I'll take you down with my tai kwon do, then stomp your gut with my kung fu till you puke blood. You think I give a damn about your thousand dollars? I'd rather watch you die for 18 minutes.'"

The editor let the piece through, untouched. "That's how you handle 'em," declares Pete, dusting off another brew, whilst clanking his shot glass on the table. It was true—Pete LeSand threatened to kill nearly every editor and agent he'd ever worked with, perhaps for justifiable reasons.

Pete identified himself in the author bio underneath his article as a "writer-fighter from Hell's Kitchen." This made him unique among Manhattan's sorry manhood. Real estate developers had renamed his area Clinton, to make it more palatable for milquetoasts, rebuffing the old melting-pot image of Hell's Kitchen. Pete's insistence on using Hell's Kitchen reflected his hell-bent resistance to gentrification.

Now, certain dames may go for soapbox orators, but Elsa was eyeing me kind of funny. She invites me back to her place to show her newest paintings.

"I'd love to," Pete interjects. Elsa picks up the tab, which contains four times as many drinks for Pete than any of us.

"Alaska," she winks at me.

Out on Eighth Avenue, Pete is feeling his oats. He promptly grabs the first Arab newsdealer behind a kiosk by the scruff of the collar.

"You cannot win," he says in a mystical voice to the little fellow. "I'm going to hypnotize you. The Moslems have no chance in the Middle East. Your whole towel-head, goat-cock-sucking religion will go down in utter defeat. Israel will endure." He moves his fingers hypnotically around the confused man's face.

I tap Pete's shoulder, reminding him the newsdealers are *Pakistani*, not Palestinian, but his drunk is in full flight.

The gals hail us a cab for the Village, and since he is sitting up front, I ask Pete to pay the driver. But Elsa beats him to it before he reaches his pocket, and he is much obliged.

Elsa has a ground-floor flat in Greenwich Village that is hard to come by these days. Though she's co-starred in a dozen X-rated films, there's not a poster in sight, not even one of her magazine covers, as some starlets of her genre like to display. Instead her walls are crowded with paintings and art objects, made by herself. She wants everyone to know that, in real life, she's an artist first and foremost, with political feminist undertones.

Elsa lays out a cold bottle of Roderer Cristal along with a hefty vial of what she calls the "finest Alaskan snow." I decline this generous offer, not wanting to mix work and play. But the writer-fighter obliges, lining up fat rows of powder which he disposes of with the snout of an aardvark.

"I'm gonna start boxing again in Brooklyn with Bennie," Pete announces to the girls, downing his glass of champagne. "I need to get my body long, hard, sinewy and dangerous. I want to write all day, then spar and train four hours with Bennie at Gleason's Gym, that's all. I feel like a god after four hours of fighting, it turns me into a warrior to deal with the rat race. Write and fight, write and fight. They can oppress me, keep me down and broke, but they will not silence me."

Margaret Letsky has not a ripple in her makeup. Her hair, pouffed with

WRITE & FIGHT   99

Dippity-Do in a blonde ponytail, is just a tad too cute, considering she's no spring chicken. She left the burlesque biz one year ago, after discovering her likeness on a 25-cent packet of vending machine condoms at a bus depot. She tries to appear interested in Pete's opinions, but sips her champagne with a stiff upright formality.

"Why do I train?" Pete asks the gals. "I train to achieve the energy of a bull, the serenity of a Buddha, the liquidity of a forest fire. That's what I need to overcome the tremendous obstacles of my chosen profession. Write and fight, that's what I do each day."

Pete spent five years in a Zen Buddhist monastery after his novel was published. After emerging, he blended his own brew of Eastern philosophies, martial arts, boxing, Talmudic study, literature, militant politics, and bullshit artistry into his own divide-and-conquer ethic. But basically, all combined, it has just enabled him to survive, so far. He was up at the crack of dawn to sit Zen for 30 minutes. Then he stood on his head and recited the Talmud. In the afternoon, after a day of writing, he trained at a gym. This gave him spiritual armor to deal with the ephemeral, superficial fools of the publishing industry. To face them like a warrior, in an establishment out to crush serious writers and everything they stood for. With this I had no argument. But how boxing skills translated into sharper prose remained abstract.

Pete rises to his feet, announcing we are in a state of emergency. Corporate terrorists in the real estate war have crushed the middle and lower classes. He stands upon Elsa's ottoman to explain how a handful of mean, nasty industries have bought out most of the book and magazine companies, merging into a monopoly. The corporate monster was crushing every breath of virtuous, heartfelt prose, replacing it with supermarket pablum. Once-great magazines were now whorish ad supplements, their very covers pandering subliminally to young white wealth.

"They hate me!" expounds Pete, standing big above us, shaking his fist. "They hate what I stand for, they despise art. I'm one tiny voice, I'm nothing, I can't stand up to their 80-story towers of shit that they erect on every block I once loved."

Again, I have no argument with Pete's view. But he inhales the last of the Alaskan, and bellows at the poor porno girls.

"Nobody raises more than an eyebrow, they say it's fate! The corporate monster tramples our city, our whole country, crushing every morsel of Americana and soul and humanity, and nobody does anything!

"Only 12 people march against Lyndon LaRouche when he campaigns in New York. Here is a veiled neo-Nazi party that could become a third contender in the next election. There are 20 million in the tri-state area, and only 12 show up to protest outside LaRouche's hotel in Manhattan. 12!"

Indeed, Pete's fist made the six o'clock news the night before, leading the march. Pete's face freezes in a look of incredulity as Elsa carries out an armful of fresh paintings she did of Klondike Maggie. Maggie is a fellow whore on dogsled who swoops down to relieve indigent pipelayers from all over America who came to Alaska for stout wages and adventure. The paintings are somewhat abstract, or perhaps I miss the point. But Ms. Kay seems to regress to the expression of a satisfied kindergarten finger-painter. One canvas appears to me blank white, but she assures us it is of an Alaskan landscape.

Pete is helping himself to more from Elsa's liquor cabinet, for which he is much obliged. He shames me for not attending yesterday's rally. Elsa chimes in the belief that her appearances on the porn screen are actually political feminist statements. This is why her university-president father has disowned her. Peter, who has switched his allegiance among quite a number of exalted teachers, proselytizes Zen until we all nearly pass out. I help him into a cab uptown.

The next afternoon, when Pete recovers, he shows up at my desk behind the harness-race score board in the back of the *Dirt* newsroom.

"Why did you try to slough me off on that broad?" he asks, incensed. Truly, I don't make sense of his accusation, or why it would be so terrible to slough someone off on a doll like Ms. Elsa Kay.

"Sure you did," he says, getting madder. "Is that how low you think of me, to go for a trashy porno whore?"

Pete usually falls for Sephardic ballerinas, female cops or women of the Israeli Defense Force. He seems truly disturbed over our evening with the porno queens.

"Those women are exploited slaves," he complains, "too stupid to pull themselves out... By the way, what's her number? I'd like to apologize for your behavior."

Here is where yours truly, with supposed 42nd-Street know-how, makes a *faux pas* in spades. Never give out a lady's number. But in the rush of the moment, I do, and Pete storms out.

It is no coincidence that two days later, a letter arrives from Elsa Kay. She too has disowned me:

"I found your friend Pete," she writes, "an insufferable pig, loudmouthed, opinionated and a buffoon. He was greedy with my liquor and coke. That you would offend me to such a degree by trying to slough him off on me, when you know I like you, is a terrible insult. Secondly, giving out a lady's phone number is unforgivable. Obviously, you have trouble handling yourself with a porn star of my caliber, which is over your head."

I do not blame the poor girl, and plead guilty as charged, though I still can't figure why she thinks I tried to slough Pete off on her. Furthermore, I've never been sure that she liked me until this letter. But I feel pity for Pete, and whatever holy hell he caught when he dared to call her.

So much a chewing-out does Pete receive from Elsa, I figure, that he won't even speak to me. When Pete hands in his cover story on Bennie at the *Daily Dirt*, he does not answer my hello, nor see see me when I walk by. I have become invisible. And so I remain for the next month, with Pete giving me the silent treatment.

Pete does not even see me at the Melody Burlesk one evening, when I make my usual rounds. I figure it odd to spot Pete in a joint he feels is beneath the pride of real men. Elsa Kay also happens to be on the showcard, one of seven "Melody Favorites" tonight. But Pete seems more rattled by the presence of three Hasidic Jews in the audience. It is a known fact that the Hasidim strictly forbids its members entry to burlesque halls. That is why whenever a bearded Hasid comes in here, he stops first and asks Mumbles behind the box office, "Are any of my people here?" If so, he leaves posthaste.

Nevertheless, there are three Hasidim sitting together in the shadows of the last row. Pete LeSand is calling them out into the aisle, his voice full of fury. "You hypocritical bastards," he yells, "how dare you show up here in sacred costume?"

The three are humiliated, afraid to open their mouths. "Get back to Williamsburg!" he demands, pulling them by the beard out of their seats, and hustling them out of the theater.

This is no shock for me to see, for Pete LeSand has a strong conscience, enough to consider himself a self-appointed watchdog. And I'm not even certain he is Jewish. Once, at a diner, I saw him challenge a police officer who'd picked up his BLT on rye at the counter without paying.

"Free cop food, free cop food!" yelled LeSand, to the whole diner. The befuddled officer had never been confronted this way.

"What's this, graft?" asked Pete. "I didn't see you pay."

"I have an arrangement," said the cop, handling it wrong, on the defensive.

It is a month since Pete has spoken to me, when I cross the oddest item in the back pages of the paper. For there in the matrimonials is an announcement of the engagement of one Pete LeSand, star *NY Dirt* reporter, and Elsa Kay, impressionist painter. The item also congratulates Pete for selling "Bennie the Benevolent" to Paramount. I'm told by an office mole that the two have moved in together. Their bond is rooted in a mutual disdain toward me for sloughing them off on each other.

Now Pete is no ponce—that is, a subservient road manager/boyfriend for the career of some stripper. Most of these guys are ex-garage mechanics who suddenly become experts of show biz, as they "manage" their girlfriend's career. But their most important function is making sure the girl's costume is back from the cleaner in time for the show. No, Pete was a great reformer who'd taken on the impossible task of setting Elsa Kay straight.

The next day I am awakened by an afternoon phone call. It is none other than Pete LeSand. He is terribly upset, and needs to meet with me immediately. I remind him I don't exist, I am invisible, but Pete insists the matter is urgent.

We meet at Jimmy Ray's Saloon that night, where Pete lines up the shot glasses. I ask what is the trouble.

"Well," begins Pete, "Paramount made me a great offer for the rights to

'Bennie.' A huge sum, which I can't reveal. They have a major name lined up for the lead, but I'm not at liberty to tell that, either."

That's good news, I say, but ask Pete why he calls not to tell me anything.

"Wait," says Pete. "They want me to do a script fast, for even more bucks. So my agent approves the contract, which is all signed. But then Bennie calls. He wants 90 percent of the take. Can you believe that?"

Peter further laments that Bennie's 90-percent demand includes Pete's screenplay fee—which, after agent's commission, lawyers, taxes and Bennie's share, would leave Pete owing quite a bit of dough. Pete has tried to explain all this math to the dock worker, but Bennie has vowed to castrate Pete, though in less polite terminology.

"It'll take months to even write the script," says Pete, head in hands. "Doesn't that lunk understand that I created a storyline out of the events of his life? That I painstakingly crafted every line of prose and turned his life into great literature?"

I guess he doesn't understand, I tell Pete.

"He makes great money. I've never made anything till this," continues Pete. "But he won't even bargain with me. I tell you, they're trying to crush us!"

Pete thought Bennie was a great friend, and he is shocked at how cutthroat Bennie is when it comes to business. Pete even told Bennie he was stopping the whole project. But several of Bennie's associates showed up at Pete's door, saying they might kill him and make it last 30 minutes if he doesn't follow through. Bennie likes the idea of movie immortality.

"I need a place to hide for a while," pleads Pete, his face turning white. "I can't even stay at Elsa's. She hooked for Bennie's union boss, they know where she lives."

I can only suggest one place to hide for Pete, until things cool down, as all things do. Since he has not settled on a honeymoon location, he can kill two birds with one stone. A long respite at the Alaska pipeline is the perfect choice for Pete and Elsa's honeymoon, since there will be need for lots of cooling down in their marriage.

Pete orders his plane tickets from the bar payphone.

—1988

CHAPTER ELEVEN

THE MAN WHO LOVED SLUT DANCING

A while back, Fred and I got to talking about the national pastime of whacking off to television. There were no surveys on the phenomenon in those days, but we figured millions of lazy slobs vegetated upon their damp couches, peckers a-dangle, transfixed on the images of gorgeous women for masturbatory accompaniment. At least to Fred and me, this non-activity revealed itself to have been quite a hobby.

We worked nine-to-five for a company that had seen better days. Our daily reminiscences hurried its descent, as we obsessively recalled famous women we had jerked off over during our blissful, though painfully secret, days as young teenage masturbators. We began compiling Top-10 lists, then a Top 40, and eventually came up with some 300 names. The rest of the office failed to see the significance of this project, as we set back the work schedule for everyone. My top five, for instance, taking into account overall appeal, the amount of times I fantasized over them, and the desire to reuse them, were approximately thus: Tuesday Weld, Jane Fonda, Brigitte Bardot, Marilyn Monroe and Mary Tyler Moore. Fred's were Joan Collins, Joey Heatherton, Sophia Loren, Angie Dickinson and the mother in the *Please Don't Eat the Daisies* TV series, in that order. His all-time favorite scene to "beat off" over was from *Inn of the Frightened People*, when young Joan Collins ravishes a younger boy, accounting for dozens of Fred's finest ejaculations. The flick was repeated often on late-night, where Fred, who scoured each week's *TV Guide* for it, waited with his Kleenex box, timing his rhythm for 35 minutes into the film, when Collins slinked out. "You knew she really did it," insisted Fred, referring to Joan's penchant for compromising her virtue in real life. No awareness had Fred of Joan Collins' current notoriety—only her B-movie days provided the fodder for his fondest TV splatterings, like *Land of the Pharaohs* and *Rally 'Round the Flag, Boys*.

But when Fred bared his soul, he confided that his greatest weakness was for something he called the "Slut Dance." When Joey Heatherton breaks bad in *Twilight of Honor*, shutting her eyes and sashaying to jukebox jungle rhythms in the diner, heating up her boyfriend. "That's what it's all about," contended Fred. "They should market those excerpts in peep shows, it'd make porn obsolete." A premature ejaculator, Fred came instantly while viewing this, or any woman lost in abandon with her eyes closed, oblivious to social taboos, casting off garments. Anita Ekberg in *Screaming Mimi*. Bardot and Jeanne Moreau in *Viva Maria*. The Slut Dance, however, had but one true queen:

"Joey, Joey, Joey," moaned Fred, unable to work behind his desk, still haunted by her sultry pout in such forgotten flicks as *My Blood Runs Cold* and *Where Has Love Gone*. "Oh, why did her tits have to be so pancakey when she finally revealed them in *Bluebeard*?"

The daughter of bandleader Ray Heatherton, who accompanied Bob Hope in leotards aboard ship to torture the troops in Nam. "Joey Heatherton represented America's last golden age, the blonde, blue-eyed slut-girl of the Kennedy years. Joey stood at the forefront of the New Frontier."

It was a day later when Fred stormed my office in a panic. "Jesus! Joey on the *Mike Douglas Show* doing exercises! In the early '70s when she guest-starred all week—I'd wait till 4:30 with a box of Kleenex, hoping my mother wouldn't call me down to an early supper, or my sister wouldn't walk in. She'd open the show with a new exercise, then you'd wait an hour till her hot song number. I even beat off to her Serta Perfect Sleeper commercials."

"On the spot?" I wondered. "That would only give you 30 seconds."

"I'd make it by the 29th."

Fred had recently turned 30 and was set to marry a brunette anthropologist whose parents had survived Auschwitz. "I see a long, parched desert before me," Fred would moan, envisioning the rest of his sex life. "Judy and I are so familiar after living together five years. I love her, but sex with her is like having sex with a family member. I'm a starving man."

Indeed, Fred's most indignant complaint about the folly of mankind was his inability to resist temptation. Hip-swaggering harlotry, a cleavage thrust in his direction, even the slightest overt female wiggle—these sights sent him careening off to relieve himself into a Kleenex in Times Square. Then he could focus on more immediate matters of digestion, seltzer water and a good bowel movement. But when particularly aroused by some sexy temp in the office, wantonly gyrating her hips while listening to a Sony Walkman, he would sneak off to the streetwalkers that night, cursing under his breath about the power women hold over men's libidos. "It's not fair," he said, pounding a fist on the table, unable to relax until he boffed a whore. And God forbid Judy should find out; it would crush her beyond repair. "Not that she'd react violently, but those doe-like eyes would swell with tears, she'd stare at me with disbelief... It's the camps," said Fred, referring to her parents' incarceration, which loomed over their relationship like a poltergeist. "You can't cheat on the daughter of concentration camp victims."

"Surely," I ventured, "you could explain your craving for a meaningless one-nighter." I suggested she may become bored too, and someday, after gentle prodding, might allow a girlfriend to slip under the covers with both of them.

"Are you crazy?" screamed Fred, whose maddest desire was for several of Judy's associate anthropologists.

"Why not try?" I asked

"The camps, the camps."

No, Fred was resigned to a lifetime of masturbation and $20 blowjobs on the sly. He confided one day that he began his curious career as a young TV whack-off artist over the dreamy, blue-jeaned Jane in *F-Troop*.

"Major league," I agreed, "but she never showed flesh."

"Yeah, but the tight jeans, they were enough," Fred countered. "I scoured the planet for anything else she might have done, but couldn't find her. She was even better than Ellie Mae Clampett."

"Ellie Mae was great," I remembered, "a fine potential climax, until Granny popped up on screen to spoil it. That's why I preferred the *Li'l Abner* girls. Remember Julie Newmar?"

"Yes, yes," screamed Fred, "Julie Newmar was fantastic, I beat off to her *Batman* episode many times, when she came out in leather as Catwoman. What fuck meat!"

"Morticia on the *Addams Family* and Marilyn on *The Munsters* were hot, but they never gave you anything to work with," I said.

"I could never score with them either," admitted Fred, "and I still feel like I'm missing something."

Thinking back to our mid-teens, we both agreed that a Saturday night date with a favorite "beat-off queen" on the telly was nearly as exciting as a genuine date, and less threatening. During a few prime teenage years there, my own eyes burned over each week's TV listings in search of Jane Fonda, Brigitte Bardot and Tuesday Weld—though Tuesday was also my favorite actress, humbling me to celibacy instead of going through with a whack-off ritual. She burst through bad material like *Lord Love A Duck* and displayed a cross-eyed magnificence in *I Walk the Line* and her greatest film, *Pretty Poison*. I tried to exercise restraint—except when Tuesday appeared as cheerleader in her one season of *Dobie Gillis*: big-league bang off!

Fred had the hots for European actresses—Jean Seberg, Virna Lisi, Romy Schneider, Leslie Caron, Claudia Cardinale, Monica Vitti, Catherine

Deneuve—any of the wives or girlfriends of Roger Vadim would do. "Sophia Loren in *Two Women*," said Fred, his eyeballs doubling in size behind his glasses, "when she and her daughter are raped side by side, and you only see their faces. She gasps to the daughter to just hang on, they'll survive. A beat-off masterpiece!"

"Liv Ullman and Bibi Andersson, when she retells the gang-rape in *Persona*," I reminded him. "The whole world jerked off to that... You never smacked off to Cybill Shepherd, I hope?"

"No, she's too untalented for me to waste my scum over," said Fred. "Models never did it for me." I breathed a sigh of agreement, which ruled out the likes of Jean Shrimpton, Twiggy, Marisa Berenson, Cheryl Tiegs, Lauren Hutton... We both admitted to having compromised on this category, however.

I'd once wanted to keep a time log of the greatest sex scenes in the pantheon of late-night movies, but lacked the obsessive mental illness of a true pervert. Instead, I'd keep an approximate mental record—45 minutes into *Tammy and the Doctor*, say, Sandra Dee's rump might hover appetizingly over the swamp, the best you'd see her all film long. Or an hour into *Barefoot in the Park*, when Jane Fonda climbs the stepladder wearing a heavenly bra, her flanks jutting out of her skimpy skirt each time she stretches. Channel 7 occasionally neglected to edit out nude scenes in Bardot films like *Les Femmes*, which sent me into outer space, as did Natalie Wood's near-nude romping in *Bob & Carol & Ted & Alice*.

Fred was a true maestro who stood before his TV set in a robe, a great conductor about to make music with his dangling pecker, the Kleenex box atop a music stand. Fred's head peered around my door, out of breath, with a revelation. "The wife on the *Mr. Ed* show! I beat off to her almost as much as the mom in *Please Don't Eat the Daisies*." Then something else hit him like a thunderbolt: "Leslie Uggams on *Sing Along with Mitch*. She was Black, you knew she *did* it!"

"How 'bout *Lawrence Welk*?" I shot back. "Some real beauts I spanked the monkey to."

"No way," said Fred. "But I could come over Cher, two, three times in one hour of the *Sonny & Cher Show*." No doubt about it, Fred was a slut-meat man, while I tended to lean toward the wholesome ones: Marlo Thomas in a few hot *That Girl*s was fair game, as was Liz Montgomery in *Bewitched*, or her younger appearances in *Thriller* and *Al Hitchcock Presents*. (Barbara Eden in *I Dream of Jeannie* left us both limp.) The older sis in *Father Knows Best* was utterly pornographic, especially whilst suntanning her white-bread legs. Even a few highlights from the *Gidget* trilogy provided wild solo sex, whether Sandra Dee, Sally Field or Karen Valentine was at the helm. (Annette Funicello movies were so bad, they left us both limp.) Karen Valentine, I ventured, was an untapped cherubic resource as a yank-off queen, appearing in such atrocities as *Love, American Style*, *Love Boat* and *The Girl Who Came Gift-Wrapped*, with the late Richard Long.

"You're sick," came Fred, hitting me with Angie Dickinson in *Police Woman* (he 'gasmed 100 times), Diana Rigg on *The Avengers* (one of the greats), Barbara Feldon of *Get Smart* (maybe once) and Ann Francis as *Honey West*—"Chalk her up for 20 shots of jism."

We were both always open to experimentation, stuff off the beaten path. Oddball jerk-off subjects could take the form of Sandy Duncan (once in some screwball TV movie, post eye-loss), Liza Minnelli in *The Sterile Cuckoo* once (this I regret), Doris Day several times (embarrassing), Patty Duke (was it Helen Keller?), Miss Jane of *Romper Room* (she was crawling on the floor), and Rita Moreno in *Electric Company*, dolled up as a teenybopper, singing about the syllable "ick" ("I get a kick out of..."). This I make no apologies for. The young Moreno was killer—lucky Brando had her as girlfriend from age 18–26. I tried once over Miss McGillicuddy (Jackie Cooper's dickthrob teach in the early *Our Gangs*), but no dice; even a jail-bait attempt over Little Rascal Darla and a weird experimental yank over cartoon Olive Oyl.

"Ever beat off to Cloris Leachman?" asked Fred.

"Naw, I'd be too scared."

"Scared of what, that you'd like it?"

In late-night moments of desperation, after hours of watching shit, I was known to slap it o'er *Lilias, Yoga and You*, in a race before the National Anthem. My most desperate attempt was over Billie Jean King one night, for which I've felt awful about ever since. This is not to say that I was guy who'd settle for just anything. I had at least some pride, some dignity. Never Bette Midler. Never Florence Henderson or the Gabor sisters, and I wouldn't have done the honor to Shelley Winters, no matter how heralded a svelte Hollywood beauty she was in the 1940s. I would've been scared shitless to even attempt it, knowing the heifer she turned into.

"You're depriving yourself," claimed Fred, "you should sail right in with the young Shelly Winters."

"You never sunk to Barbara Walters?" I asked.

"Yes, I admit, a couple of times when she presented awards and her cleavage showed. I even jerked off to the sisters in *The Brady Bunch*. I mean, that's what they're there for, right?"

"Just doing your job."

"I beat myself raw to Tina Louise on *Gilligan's Island*," said Fred. "She was a great favorite, even Mary Ann. The show was horrible, you had to work fast and make your getaway."

"Cheryl Ladd on the *The Muppets*," I put forth, "was worth a few cannon blasts of jizz, especially when she did her Stan Laurel impression."

"Couldn't be as hot as Rita Moreno's episode. She didn't do a Slut Dance, by any chance?" asked Fred.

These were all important women who figured prominently in our arrested adolescent development. Actresses with unique personalities, voices, bodies and enough raw talent to have scissored (or fucked) through tons of red tape to make it in Hollywood. But how about the thousands of anonymous beauties who made only momentary movie appearances, unable to sustain long careers, to reach even the modest achievements of a Sheree North, Marilyn Maxwell or Tippi Hedrin? Fred and I recognized their talent and paid just tribute to Tits & Ass queens like Lee Meredith, the bimbo nurse in *The Sunshine Boys*, who took dictation in *The Producers*. Elaine Joyce, fab musical comedy and cheesecake star of such Broadway shows (another category) as *Sugar*.

"The blonde lass in *Svengali*," I said. "John Barrymore gets her naked on the pedestal. She jumps off and you see her body for a split second. I timed it right only once."

"Freeze frame," said Fred, "if we only had freeze frame then!" No telling what ingenious methods today's video wankers have come up with. But we agreed we'd rather shine off over a hundred creamable, cheesecake Hollywood starlets (too obscure to list here) before doing it over one modern-day porn starlet. Did Fred take strippers seriously?

"Yeah, once beat off to a panel of old strippers on the *Suskind* show. Gypsy Rose Lee related a story about how she told a dozen guys in the front row who were beating off, 'Are ya ready yet, fellas, or can you use another 12 bars?'"

Horror movie vamps?

"Don't even get me started on Barbara Steele," revealed Fred. "I beat my dick to a pulpy noodle."

English actresses, it turned out, provided a dizzying masturbatory flavor for both of us, Fred in particular. He had drained his body of jism for years over Charlotte Rampling in *Georgy Girl* and *The Night Porter*, Julie Christie in *Darling* and *Petunia*, Jackie Bisset, Sara Miles, Samantha Eggar, Hayley Mills. And neither of us felt threatened by aggressive go-getter women in old movies. No, we charged right in with clenched fist over Babs Stanwyck's bad-girl roles in the '40s. Kate Hepburn being carried from the pool in *Philadelphia Story*, or her massage in *Pat and Mike* ("cherce" meat, says Spencer). Jean Arthur was ferociously sexy, and the towel-clad Donna Reed was a cocktease in *It's a Wonderful Life*. (Garbo left us limp.) Moving on into the '50s, Fred and I yanked off profusely to standards like Monroe, Mansfield and Grace Kelly. "It was practically the law, you had to," said Fred.

Audrey Hepburn was splendid, and Debbie Reynolds heavenly, in the Top 10 on both our lists. Anything with the young Ann-Margret was, of course, smack-off city. Then there was a parade of beauties in their prime who we polished off over, like Lee Remick, Suzanne Pleshette, Dorothy Provine, Janice Rule, both the Carroll Baker and Carol Lynley versions of *Harlow*. Whole boxes of Kleenex over Katherine Ross and the young (only the young) Candice Bergen. Stella Stevens, Connie Stevens and Inger Stevens. "Oh, why did Inger have to commit suicide?" cried Fred, his spirits wilting.

After all the names we came up with, we agreed they only scratched the surface. Consider the whole spectrum of masturbatory memories: early babysitters who fell asleep on your couch; the teacher who exiled you under her desk for an hour, as punishment; *Playboy* and *Cavalier*, which were dynamite to an adolescent lad in the 1960s; other people's family photo albums. I admitted to feeling a charge at the sight of a lady's spilled pocketbook contents, and Fred had a high old time with his sister's Tampax directions.

It was now that I confessed my greatest fantasy. Fred was all ears. The hottest sight of all time, I explained, was the young Mary Tyler Moore as suburban housewife on *The Dick Van Dyke Show*. So go figure the mysteries of attraction. Fred thought this was pathetic.

The inimitable, lovable, crotch-exploding, oil-wells-of-jizz-producing Laura Petrie! As an adolescent, I'd shoot a mile, a hot shot that could not only hit the fence, but burn it down. Laura Petrie was padded-bra ecstasy, in pumps and Capri slacks that set the standard for the modern suburban housewife. (She was a real-life diabetic who hid her bad posture in sweaters.) Nevertheless, I'd wipe the steam off my TV set as she vacuumed the rug while the great Dick Van Dyke was down at the office, writing gags with Morey Amsterdam. I wanted to chew Laura Petrie's panties right off, drink her bath water, take a swan dive into her laundry hamper. To steal her from Dick V.D. and that ugly kid, and worship her like the suburban goddess she was. And ultimately, to settle down, have some kids, get bored... and watch reruns of *The Mary Tyler Moore Show*.

Fred was struck dumb.

"... She didn't happen to ever do a Slut Dance, by any chance?"

Our conversations came to an abrupt halt one day. Fred was getting fidgety. "Hey, this stuff is private, our innermost secrets, just between us, right?" he asked. "Ya know," he concluded, "they just don't make TV shows to jerk off to like they used to. Today's cable shows are too easy, too obvious. Anyone can beat off to a porn flick, big deal."

"'Twas an art, jerking off to *My Little Margie*," I finished.

—1984

...IN TEXAS

CHAPTER TWELVE

JACK RUBY: DALLAS' ORIGINAL J.R.

Jack Ruby would have turned 80 on March 25, 1991. I tried to gather a round table of former Ruby strippers for this occasion. After much detective legwork, I could not turn up one aging broad—all of Ruby's girls had vanished into the smoke of assassination lore. What follows instead are reminiscences of friends, foes, musicians and acquaintances who were still at large.

He is frozen in our consciousness as the charging, black-suited patriot who gunned down Oswald on national TV two days after Kennedy's death. Ruby believed he avenged his president's murder, saved Dallas' reputation in the eyes of the world, made the Jews look good and spared fair Jacqueline the horror of a murder trial.

Jack Ruby has figured in countless conspiracy theories, works of fiction and history books. He remains a star player in the American mythology of the JFK Assassination. A librarian at the Dallas Public Library refers tiredly to the huge assassination file log as "the Kennedy junk." In 1990, Ruby's executor-attorney was asking $130,000 for the .38 Colt Cobra that killed

Oswald, along with some mundane possessions, like an undershirt Jack bought at Sears. (Who the hell would desire Jack Ruby's undershirt?)

An international glare came upon Jack Ruby's dark little corner of Dallas night life on November 25, 1963. His second-rate strip joint, the Carousel, became the world's most famous burlesque. Yet few customers ventured in after Ruby hit the front pages.

"Anybody coulda killed Oswald, the way people's feelings was running at that time—it didn't surprise me it was Jack," says Dallas Deputy Sheriff Lynn Burk, who knew Ruby well and was present when Oswald was captured at the Texas Theater. "I'm surprised some policeman didn't kill Oswald first."

"He stuck by what he did," says Captain Ray Abner, who was Ruby's personal jail guard. "He said he loved Kennedy and that he was glad he did it. But I believe Jack just intended to wound Oswald. Spend a couple years in prison, sell a book and movie rights. He was a small figure who came up from the Chicago underworld. He was a guy who wanted to be a big shot."

On Ruby's last day as a free citizen that November morning in '63, he was a paunchy, balding, 52-year-old burly-Q operator. He had oily, slicked-back black hair, a cleft in his chin, five-o'clock jowl shadow, and he wore cuff links, a tie stickpin and diamond pinky rings.

The Carousel was located downtown on Commerce Street, one flight up, between a parking garage and a short-order restaurant. Strippers' 8x10's hung over the entrance. A $2 cover allowed horny patrons entrance to a square, barn-like room with dark red carpeting and booths of black plastic. Jack Ruby's stage was the size of a boxing ring, with a five-piece bump-and-grind orchestra, but no dancing. The bar was boomerang-shaped, finished in gold-plated plastic and gaudy gold-mesh drapes. The Black barkeep, Andy Armstrong, was Ruby's right-hand man. Overhead hung a gold-framed painting of a stallion, which Ruby believed had "real class."

Obsessed with "class," he operated from a dingy little office in the back with a gray metal desk and small safe.

Terré Tale, a Dallas strip queen of the '60s, had a dozen routines. The crowd favorite was an Uncle Sam act in which her boobs marched in time with a hup-two-three-four soundtrack. She met Ruby when innocently answering a Carousel newspaper ad for a cocktail waitress: "The Black bartender told me to come back with the sexiest outfit I had. When I came back, they sat me down next to a guy with more arms than an octopus. I didn't even know the Carousel had strippers. I'd never *seen* a strip. The girls laughed at my reaction. 'When Jack sees you, he'll have you on amateur night this Friday.' But Jack Ruby was nice to me. 'Does your body look as good as your face?' he said. 'No, I have two kids,' I told him. Then he told me he could make me a star, put me in an apartment, send me to the beauty parlor every day."

Terré Tale refused Ruby's offer, but a few years later she was headlining the Colony Club, two doors down from Ruby at 1322 Commerce. Abe Weinstein's Colony Club was Dallas's most reputable burlesque from 1939 to 1973. Ruby envied this deco cabaret, which seemed to possess the elusive class he so craved.

"My club was a nightclub," says retired owner Abe Weinstein, now 83. "His was just a joint. I had big names; he had nobody. When he came from Chicago to Dallas in '47, he came up to my club right away. He was told there's a Jew runs a club, that's how I met him."

Ruby, whose God-given name was Rubenstein, ran a few music spots before opening the Carousel right next to Abe in 1960. Ruby was a tremendous pain in the ass, bottom-feeding off the Colony's action for three years. "My relationship with Jack was bad," says Weinstein. "He threatened to kill me one week before he killed Oswald. I'd had him barred from the club. He tried to hire away my waitresses and employees. Here's my opinion: Jack Ruby killed Oswald because he wanted to be world-famous. If he'd have killed Oswald before the police got Oswald, he would have been a hero. But it was no great thing to get him in the police station."

Ruby was particularly jealous of amateur night at the Colony and the lines it drew. There was no such thing as jail bait—girls in their mid-teens could hop onstage and strip.

"I started when I was 15," recalls former stripper Bubbles Cash in her North Dallas jewelry-pawn shop, Top Cash. "If you were married in Texas, you could do anything your husband said you could do. I married at 13. I told my husband I wanted to be a dancer and take Candy Barr's place as a star in downtown Dallas. The ladies were like movie stars, glamorous, classy. The first time I took my clothes off onstage was great. I wore a red, white and blue dress, and when I unzipped, everyone went crazy, and my husband was proud. It was amateur night."

Eventually Ruby ripped off the amateur-night idea, sweet-talking local secretaries who'd never gotten naked before an audience onto the Carousel stage.

Bubbles recoils at the mention of Ruby, whom she never worked for: "I was told by Abe don't even go near his place. The Carousel had a bad connotation; the girls weren't on their best behavior. They did some hookin' outta there."

Weinstein, who lives alone with his memories, has almost no contact today with any of the strippers who graced his establishment. "I had *the* biggest stripper, Candy Barr," boasts Weinstein. She was another figure associated in myth with Ruby. Abe pronounces her name with the same emphasis one would use for a Milky Way candy bar. "I named her, started her in the business, managed her. She packed the house every night."

Abe claims Barr never worked for Ruby or had anything to do with him. But according to sax player Joe Johnson, Candy Barr came after hours to Ruby's Vegas Club, in the late '50s, to strip. "All the girls came over to the Vegas to strip," says Johnson, who led a five-piece R&B group there. Johnson worked for Ruby six years, starting in 1957. His trademark was belting out sax solos as he walked along the bar top. "I was part of a family. Ruby was the best boss I had in Dallas. After he shot Oswald, the FBI followed me everywhere I'd play. I got six pages in the Warren Report."

Legendary Dallas-born Big Texas Tenor, David "Fathead" Newman, took hometown gigs at Ruby's Vegas and Silver Spur dives, when on leave from Ray Charles. "The thing I remember most about Jack Ruby," chuckles Newman, "were the stag parties in his clubs. Whenever the striptease dancers came out, he'd want the musicians to turn our backs, 'cause these were white ladies. He'd say, 'Now, you guys turn your backs so you can't see this.' But the strippers would insist that the drummer watch them so he could catch their bumps and grinds. So, Jack says, 'Well, the drummer can look, but the rest of you guys, you turn your backs on the bandstand.'"

Ruby's penchant for barroom brawls kept him in minor scrapes with Texas law. Deputy Sheriff Lynn Burk, a dapper 67, remembers the frontier days of Naughty Dallas. He was a frequent lunch mate of Ruby's, and still has Jack's Riverside phone number in his phone book. Burk ironed out some of Ruby's barroom troubles.

He first entered Ruby's music joint, the Silver Spur, in 1953: "Jack was stayin' open late; there was suspicion he was serving liquor after hours." Working undercover, Burk visited the club with a pint of whiskey and poured himself a shot in the wee hours. Ruby politely told him to take it outside, thus abiding by the law. Burk was impressed.

Pre-Kennedy Assassination Dallas had small-town camaraderie, whereby the Texas Liquor Control Board supervisor could meet for lunch with a burlesque owner. Ruby often brought sandwiches by the dozen up to police headquarters. Free drinks went to servicemen, even reporters, whom Ruby ingratiated himself with. That's why he wasn't seen as out of place in the basement where Oswald was transferred.

Burk says he enjoyed Jack's stories about a street-fighting childhood on the East Side of Chicago. Ruby had been a Chicago ticket scalper, then sold tip sheets at a California racetrack. He came to Big D after the Army discharged him in '47 with a good-conduct medal and sharpshooters rating.

Burk recalls that Ruby was a good fighter who lifted weights and sparred with former welterweight champ Barney Ross, who appeared as a character witness in Ruby's murder trial.

"When I was assistant supervisor of the Liquor Board in Dallas, a man called one day, wanted to know what we did to proprietors who beat up customers. I said you come to my office, and if we prove a breach of the peace, we can suspend his license.

"So this great, big man, well-dressed, comes in, some executive with LTV. Said he was down at the Carousel, he'd gotten separated from some friends. He thought they might have entered the Carousel, so he went up and paid admission, walked around, didn't see 'em, so he asked for his money back before leaving. They said no, wouldn't give him his money back. He said, 'Well, I'm not staying.' They said, 'Well, we're not giving your money back.' Then he said the proprietor knocked him down. He got up, and the proprietor knocked him down again.

"I said, 'I'll get Jack Ruby down here; you identify him.' I called Jack. I said, 'Come on down, and come to my office first, you understand?' Because the complainant and the supervisor were sitting in the other office.

"I said, 'Jack, there's a man in the next room you beat up at the Carousel.'

He remembered. I said, 'We're goin' in there, and you be the most humble damn man ever walked into that damn office.' So we go in, and I say, 'Mr. Smith, this is Jack Ruby.' Jack said, 'The first thing I wanna do is apologize.' The man said, 'Why did you knock me down the second time?' Jack said, 'You're a lot bigger than I am,' and described a fight where he knocked a man down once who got up and bit his finger off. Ruby showed his missing finger. He said that was the reason he always hits a man a second time. He said, 'You can bring your whole office to my club; I'll feed them and give them drinks— I'm just sorry for what happened.' The man dropped the complaint."

Abe Weinstein tells this anecdote about Ruby's temperament: "There was a famous Dallas society doctor that lived in Highland Park. He was a good customer of mine, never bothered anybody or fooled with the girls. For years, every time his wife left town, he'd come up to the Colony. Then a month passed, two months, I never saw him. I called a meeting with the girls, but nobody seen him.

"One day I'm walking by the Adolphus Hotel on Commerce, and I ran into Dr. Ross. He told me there'd been a doctors' convention in town. A colleague from Los Angeles stayed with him, and Dr. Ross showed him the city. Took him up to Ruby's place first, and he didn't like the show. Dr. Ross walked down the steps and said he'd take the guy next door for a real show. Jack Ruby happened to be standing behind and heard the remark. When they got to the bottom of the steps, Ruby grabbed Ross by the neck and knocked out all his teeth. He couldn't report it to the police because he was a Highland Park society doctor—what was he doin' in this joint?

"But that's Jack Ruby, Dr. Jekyll and Mr. Hyde. If you went into his club, he'd never seen you before, and said, 'Jack, I'm hungry; I don't have a place to sleep,' he would feed you and give you a place to sleep. But if he didn't like you, he'd stab you in the back."

Virtually all the strippers who worked for Jack Ruby have evaporated from the city of Dallas. Just try searching for a Double Delite in the phone directory. "I didn't live 47 years by talking about it," spat one ex-husband of a Ruby stripper, who hung up.

"You're talking three generations of strippers back," explains Shane Bondurant, a 1960s burlesque star who now preaches at the Rock of Ages church. Ms. Bondurant once twirled a ten-gallon Stetson hat from one boob to the next, whilst spinning two pistols at the hips. She used live snakes in her act, and made headlines when one of the two lions she kept in her trailer park bit her leg.

Like Bubbles Cash, Terré Tale and Abe Weinstein, Ms. Bondurant knows the whereabouts of not one single Ruby girl: "I would figure most became prostitutes, addicts or died. A stripper's career is ten years, and the few who survive afterward must be quite strong and pull their lives together."

Ruby's girls were not that strong. There were suicides that became part of the conspiracy lore. Baby LeGrand, whom Ruby wired money minutes before killing Oswald, was found hung by her toreador pants in an Oklahoma City holding cell in 1965. Arrested on prostitution charges, her death was ruled a suicide.

Tuesday Nite was another suicide. And in August 1990, worldwide interest was stirred by the latest conspiracy theory: The son of a Dallas cop claimed his father shot JFK, and presented a plausible scenario of evidence. His mother had worked at the Carousel, overhearing Ruby and her husband discussing the planned assassination. She was then given shock treatments, and is now allegedly too ill to speak to reporters.

Certain Ruby girls showed great devotion for their boss. Little Lynn liked Ruby enough to show up at the jail crying after Ruby was imprisoned. The 19-year-old, blue-eyed stripper carried a Beretta pistol in her scarf to give him. She was arrested at the entrance.

Shari Angel, once billed as "Dallas' own Gypsy," also kept a candle burning for Jack Ruby. In a 1986 *Dallas Times Herald* interview, the former Carousel headliner tried to raise money for "a medal or monument for Jack. He was a wonderful man." Angel described him as a mother hen to the girls, who took them to dinner and bowling. She married the Carousel emcee, Wally Weston, who later died of lung cancer. After years in an alcoholic haze, she found Jesus and pulled herself together. "You know," she told the *Herald*, "I've seen [Ruby] hit a man—I mean a real hard shot—and then pick him up and feed him for a week. He was big-hearted. If I could just get a monument to him, then maybe we could finally lay him to rest."

Angel once again relates Ruby's attack-repent ritual of belting some guy out, only to turn around and "feed" him. A little-known literary gem, *Jack Ruby's Girls*, was published in 1970 by Genesis Press in Atlanta. "In Loving Memory of Jack Ruby," read the dedication by Diana Hunter and Alice Anderson. "Our raging boss, our faithful friend, the kindest hearted sonuvabitch we ever knew." This reflected the love-hate relationship of a half-dozen strippers profiled within.

There was Tawny Angel, who Ruby fell "insanely in love with," tripping over his speech. Until her, say the authors, Jack Ruby-style sex encompassed only superficial one-nighters with "bus-station girls, trollops and promiscuous dancers."

"Jack Ruby's Carousel Club was in the heart of a city that never took the Carousel to its heart," wrote the authors. "Dumping" champagne was a Carousel ritual. Girls accidentally spilled bottles of the rotgut stuff, marked up to $17.50 from a $1.60 wholesale price. Jack Ruby beer went for 60¢ a glass, and it was shit. He encouraged the bar girls not to drink it, just to waste it when sitting with suckers in the booths. Ruby didn't allow hooking, claimed the authors, just the false promise of sex so they could hustle champagne.

Jack chiseled money from customers, yet loaned money to friends. He beat, pistol-whipped and blackjacked unruly patrons down the stairs. Spend money or get out—that was the attitude of the man who avenged President Kennedy's death.

"I never believed there was a conspiracy between Jack and anyone," states Deputy Sheriff Burk, never before interviewed about Ruby. "Because Jack Ruby had two dogs he thought more of than anybody. If he had any idea he was gonna kill Oswald, he woulda arranged for those dogs. It was a spontaneous outburst—he was over at the Western Union when they moved Oswald. It was timing."

Not many folks came to visit Ruby in jail, according to Ray Abner. Immediately following the arrest, Abner was assigned to guard Ruby's jail cell for over a year. He kept an ear on phone calls, listened to the arguments between Ruby and his sister Eva, watched him shower, heard him break mighty wind, even must have smelled it.

Ruby's cell was isolated from the rest of the prisoners, near the chief's office, with full-time security. "Jack liked special attention," says Abner. "He felt like they oughta prepare meals the way he wanted 'em. I ate strictly jail food, same as the prisoners, and I insisted he do the same. None of the girls came to see him. Just his lawyers, his sister Eva and his brother Earl. I couldn't help but overhear his conversations, so I'm pretty sure he wasn't involved in any conspiracy."

Ruby was riding high in the months after he shot Oswald. He doted over his daily shipment of fan mail, over 50 letters a day congratulating him, calling him a hero. "But after a while," Abner remembers, "the fan mail dropped off, and he got depressed."

Ruby was convicted, and he died of cancer in January 1967 while he was awaiting a retrial. In the meantime, those who made their living in his champagne-hustle world had to go elsewhere for work. *Jack Ruby's Girls* documents the pilgrimage of two strippers after the Carousel closed: Lacy and Sue Ann applied for jobs at Madame De Luce's upscale whorehouse in the Turtle Creek area of Dallas. But Madame believed Ruby "ruined" women as potential prostitutes. All tease, promise, but no fuck is what Ruby taught them. The reputation as a Ruby Girl was a stigma for those who tried to become hookers.

Jack Ruby didn't allow that type of hanky panky in the Carousel. "This is a fuckin' high-class place!" he would remind any doubting Tom, Dick or Harry, as he kicked them down the stairs.

—1990

CHAPTER THIRTEEN

THUNDER ROAD
BITES THE DUST

Driving up the bend of Jacksboro Highway, retired cowpokes squint their eyes upon a familiar landscape unchanged in 50 years. It is the sepia-toned Massey's 21 Club and the Rockwood Motel, a 1930s motor lodge, surrounded by green hills and bathed in a massive horizon. Old farmers and former Fort Worth rodeo cowboys mosey on in around happy hour. This is the same bar they've been drinking at since they were young and wild, when Jacksboro Highway was known as "Thunder Road"—a 16-mile stretch between Fort Worth and Azle, Texas.

Jacksboro Highway attracted the meanest white people in all of Texas. Outlaws hid there and gangsters flourished within the 40-odd honky-tonk beer joints and lavish nightclubs. The 16-mile stream of neon offered a proliferation of illegal slot machines, backroom gambling, whores, dope, booze and constant shootouts.

By 1990 the Highway Department will be razing Massey's 21 Club, along with most of the remaining old honky-tonks along the Jax.

Massey's was one of the safer spots. Proprietor Bobby Sitton promised his father-in-law, Hubert Massey, he'd keep the club looking the same as it did in the 1930s. He's kept his promise.

"I really don't know why," says Bobby, "but back in those days there was a lot of mean people around. 'Course, most of 'em all been thinned out. Stabbed to death, car wrecks, shot, dynamited or still in the pen from back in the old days. Very few of 'em just flat died."

Sitton, 56, grew up on the Jax, and talks friendly as apple pie. Yet he's bowlegged and battle-scarred, with knife scars across the belly. He's been shot twice in local bars and he's "got stitches on top of stitches" across his head, where countless beer bottles have crashed.

"When you own a club on the Jacksboro, you may be the owner, but you're always the bouncer," says Sitton. His hands seem constructed like large, puffy fists. He scratches his head, bewildered as to why Jacksboro was more violent than other places on Earth.

"When we were growing up out here, it just seemed like the thing to do was fighting. Mostly just good ol' fist fighting, no guns or knives. Worst thing was a beer bottle on the head. Get out there, pick a fight, have a good knockdown drag-out. I've been beat on all my life."

Th-e most troublesome problem Bobby now faces is the loss of his club and the old motel behind it, The Rockwood. Massey's rose from the base of a street car diner in 1934. It is like a western version of Sardi's on Broadway, deserving of landmark status. Red leather bar stools are built into the counter. Old silver beer refrigerators align the tender's side of the bar. The seating booths are made of cozy red leather, each fitted with a Seeburg Consolette jukebox. Massey's water still comes from a well dug out by Bobby's father-in-law. ("Best well water you ever drunk in your life," Sitton proudly points out.) His handsome mother-in-law, with a regal beehive, lends class to the joint, bantering with old customers at the bar. Today, she speaks with Billy Ray Robinson, owner of the Arabian-baroque Caravan Motel up on the corner, which his daddy and uncle built. He'll lose his land to the highway, too.

You expect Clark Gable to swagger in for a cup o' Joe, a gum-snappin' Jean Harlow to strut over and jot down your Old Bushmills order on a pad. Like most owners of rough-and-tumble joints, Bobby Sitton will sooner stress his gentle nature. His role model in the art of behaving like a gentleman was Hubert Massey, whose family also founded Fort Worth's greatest chicken-fried steak restaurant on Eighth Avenue.

"A genuine statesman and gentleman," says Bobby, who watched his father-in-law offer countless gangsters a free drink with the condition they "call it a day and leave."

"This club is a family place, where ladies wear dresses and dance to the old-fashioned waltz. We don't allow any known criminals, prostitutes or dope dealers to come in here."

On weekends, Massey's features country and western dancing to the seasoned Jacksboro Highway Band. Leon Short, the 52-year-old lead singer, is the great-great grandson of Luke Short, who gunned down Marshall Longhair Jim Courtright (a former outlaw himself) outside the White Elephant Saloon on Hell's Half Acre in Fort Worth, about two miles from the saloon's current location. "Blasted off the sheriff's thumb," says Bobby, as if he saw it, "so he couldn't shoot—then blew him away."

One of the legendary survivors of the old Jax, Cliff Helton, sits at the bar. There's a 50-year-old photo of Cliff by the cash register. He's out on the Highway, posing alongside his freshly crashed 1936 Ford, wearing a Great Gatsby suit and a movie-star smile. Folks used to refer to Cliff as the Mayor of Jacksboro Highway. He owned dozens of joints, bars, bar-B-Q's. He stood shotgun over them all, and shot off many a kneecap. They say he gambled most every one away at the flip of a card. As "one of the survivors," now in his seventies, Cliff doesn't necessarily like to talk about the old days.

"He's mellowed some," says one old-timer at the bar, "but you don't wanna fool with him. You push him in the corner, do something bad, he gonna do it back worse."

Jacksboro Highway's gang warfare of the 1950s created a situation where most of the gangsters shot themselves into extinction. Dozens received gangland executions, their bodies strewn about narrow graves by Lake Worth. Every night, some fool would walk into a bar and announce he was the "toughest man in Texas," and wait for someone to prove him wrong.

But the professional tough guys had names like Cecil Green, who was shot by gunmen in a Jacksboro nightspot while he counted an extortion haul. Sitting with him was Tincy Eggleston, who escaped the bullet hail. Tincy later had his head blown off by Gene Paul Norris, over robbery money from an alleged Cuban weapons deal. One of the last heavies to go, Norris was gunned down in 1957 by an army of Texas Rangers, state troopers and Fort Worth cops. They chased him into a field after he robbed the Carswell Air Force Base payroll.

The regulars at the last honky-tonks on the Jax still speak quietly the names of those gangsters, 25 years after the last of them were killed. But they can't figure why the highway is just now being "cleaned up," two decades later.

The gambling halls and gangster dens all died with the outlaws. But the encroaching fast-food chains that already clutter the Jax will finish off the last of the wild West. The Highway Department will carve out an eight-lane freeway of corporate shopping malls, and plow over the remnants of Thunder Road.

They will also be eliminating a cowpoke tradition that hasn't lost a moment from the days when the southeast corner of downtown Fort Worth was known as "Hell's Half Acre." It was an outlaw community unrivaled in the West. By the turn of the century there were over 80 whorehouses in business. Fannie Porter's house of ill repute harbored the Hole in the Wall Gang (Butch Cassidy and the Sundance Kid). Legend has it Bonnie and Clyde stayed in the Right Hotel on North Main Street, now called the Stockyards Hotel. In fact, the suite they are said to have slept in is named after them.

Hell's Half Acre seemed to move onto Jacksboro Highway by the 1930s. It was still mostly prairie between downtown Fort Worth and Lake Worth. The Jacksboro was built up by the state of Texas to accommodate Carswell Air Force Base and an aircraft factory, bringing thousands of soldiers and plant workers to the area. Cops called it the "Jax Beer Highway" in the '40s and '50s, where blue-collar hay hands and packing-house workers got drunk, fought and sometimes killed each other. White kids with money from the Arlington suburbs scored reefers in the back alleys, at a time when marijuana was still a dark secret of Negroes and Orientals. The honky-tonks became off-limits to Carswell personnel when it became evident that cowpokes, Yankee fliers and hay hands made for volatile bedfellows.

The bouncers could usually control the fights at the good clubs. Since World War II, the Rocket Club has been peeling back its canvas roof for summer dancing under the stars. It's now a white-washed ghost of its former self, where Mexican dances are held. The new highway will demolish it. Top Texas swing bands, including Bob Wills and his Texas Playboys, and the Light Crust Doughboys, made it out to the Jax to play such palaces as the Coconut Grove, the Skyliner and the Casino.

Bill Luttrell began playing the Highway that many country musicians avoided, at Hattie's Silver Dollar in 1946: "It was a real bad place," says the guitarist, with a hearty laugh. "Notorious for fighting. People from Azle came out there. Two women started fighting one night, then one guy tried to break 'em up and, 'course, everybody in the house jumped on him. I thought we'd never escape. We hit the window with a mike stand and crawled out. When the fight was over, we went back for our PA, which was literally destroyed.

"I played the Skyliner, the last big strip joint [which featured Dallas stripper Candy Barr], on the last night, about 20 years ago. Little Lynn was starring; she'd been part of the Jack Ruby murder trial. I don't think the police chief much liked her coming here, 'cause they raided us that night at 10 o'clock. Took all the strippers and the club owner to jail. I went down to pick him up. This was a union club, too, so we all got paid; even the strippers were union. Then the Skyliner reopened as a dance joint. The new guy that owned it wrote everybody hot checks, including the beer company, the radio station and newspaper [that ran his] ads, even Ernest Tubb, who headlined opening night."

The worst thing Luttrell remembers was the night a guitarist named Jimmy Garner went to sub for him at the Rockwood Lounge. "He got killed. He bumped into two mean drunks who got mad and stabbed him."

The big neon V out on Jacksboro is a dining landmark. Vivian Courtney's Restaurant still serves great chicken-fried *anything*. During World War II, the establishment was called Harmon's, and served more dinners by carhop than anywhere on the strip. Vivian took over in 1946.

She raised two daughters here, and curls an eyebrow suspiciously over Jacksboro's myths and legends. "Nobody ever bothered us."

"I think Mansfield Highway was just as dangerous," drawls her husband Bill, a tall, burly Texan. "For what they say happened on this highway, they coulda went to the moon. All I remember is what I did."

The Courtneys' restaurant will likely lose its locale when the freeway is built. They're not particularly sentimental and feel too old to fight it.

"Time marches on," says Bill, pointing out that 60 local chain-type businesses signed up in support of the new highway. "When the Highway Department wants our land, they'll take it."

"All I'm doin' is settin' and wonderin'," says Inez, owner of the Inez 50-50 Club, a country and western bar with hot live music. "They didn't build these new KMarts and Jack-In-The-Boxes to be torn down," she observes. Touring the strip by car, she points out how all the new fast-food stores seem strategically set more than 36 feet off the road, within legal limits to remain if a freeway cuts up the middle. If the highway goes south, they'll have to cut down KMart, bigger than a football field, which seems unlikely. If they route around north, they'll steer traffic away, leaving Inez' club in a back-road shadow. If they cut down the middle, they'll have to buy her out at "fair market prices" and raze the club.

"Once they build the new highway, business'll probably be good for a year. Then all these little neighborhood places—people gonna quit comin', they'll forget, they'll hate to get off the highway, it'll be dangerous. You know how it goes."

Inez has been on the highway since her youth. Still sexy at 70, she's on the lookout for a tenth husband. "You can't be married and run a club. You gotta marry the club.

"I've been up and down the road," she says, steering her luxury car past ghost locations. She points to an empty lot: "That's where Tincy Eggleston's gang used to hang out, a bad bunch. They blowed it up, that's why it's not there anymore. I guess they're all pretty near dead, but I don't like to say anything 'cause they have families.

"That was the Sweet Two Two Five... Up on the hill was the Chateau. After the Fort Worth Stock Show, they'd all be up here at night, playing slot machines, diceboards, girls.

"Oh, I throwed Willie Nelson outta my club many a time," she remembers, "back in '50, '51. He was married to a Mexican girl, and he worked at a service station with my baby boy. He didn't sing—he used to talk sad and play his guitar. Drove me crazy. I had a little old place called the Hayloft, and he'd set up there with his feet hangin' down. Customers'd say, 'Please get him down.' I'd say, 'Willie, they want you to get out.' He'd usually go somewhere else, till they run him off, just playin' for drinks."

30 years ago, out on the Jax, a club owner could send in $12 tax per month to the state. Now, Inez explains, it's become much harder to run a club. "I sold beer 10 cents a bottle, three for a quarter. Now for each drink I have to send 12 cents to the state. I'm audited in Austin, have to send them three thousand dollars a month.

Like other club owners on the Jax, Inez claims she never associated or did trade with gangsters. "I have never had any serious trouble at my club. I've held a license 47 years, and never had a shootin' or a cuttin'." The main troubles Inez had were good-old knock-down drag-out fights, which could only have occurred in a time of prosperity, when the country was happier. Fighting clean was a euphoric tradition, and has gone the way of drive-ins and Buffalo nickels.

"We had lots of rodeo boys, they just *loved* to fight. With their fists. They were just squares, not characters, who'd get drunk and see who's toughest. Somebody'd say he could whup anyone on the highway; next thing ya know, they'd meet up the street and make bets. Then they'd come back, buy each other beers... . But people won't fight no more, you'll get killed, they'll get a gun and come back to blow yer head off. The honor of fighting has gone. I think it's 'cause of dope, people are more worried, can't afford a night out anymore. They don't fool with fighting, just leave 'em alone or they'll kill ya.

"I'm getting old," claims Inez. "I'd like to get out of it. It's slowed down at the club, I don't think there's much goin' on now on Jacksboro Highway. They might relocate me, but I don't know where to go. Lord, yes, I will retire if they buy my place. 47 years of this is enough."

Bobby Sitton remembers Inez' place as "real dangerous, still lotsa trouble." But of Massey's he claims there hasn't been a fight in several years: "And I was involved in it myself. About 15 Irishmen come in. First time we ever had any problems with the Irish. They were filthy-mouthed, like they'd finish their beer and th'owed it behind the bar. I ordered 'em outta the place. Then one of 'em th'owed a beer in my face. Nobody th'ows no beer on *me*. I knocked the hell outta him, smacked him a damn good one, sent him all the way into the jukebox. All his friends got up, and it come out to quite a battle raw. I fought 'em all the way from here to the dance floor, got knocked down a few times myself. My wife jumped off the bar on about five of 'em. The bar girl called the law, and the po-lice got here quick, arrested some of 'em."

Bobby often visits the Oakwood Cemetery, "the most beautiful cemetery you ever seen." On the short drive to Oakwood, he proudly points out the dives of yesteryear: "Used to be a place here called Lottie's—I got shot in the arm by the bartender. We'd had a fallin' out night before, and he didn't serve me a beer, so I hit him over the head with a beer bottle. My fault. He shot me in the damn arm, I had to crawl out to keep him from shootin' again. Then he come outside and still shot at me.

"And there's the old Cartwheel Club, and boy, you talk about fightin'. There was a hellhole if there ever was one. The old man who owned it, name was Grip. Well, one night he decided I needed to leave. So I started out and the sonofagun shot me through the side. I guess I wasn't leavin' quick enough to suit him. That created a pretty good stink, 'cause I had a bunch of friends who got upset and broke all the windows out."

Bobby steps out at Oakwood Cemetery, off the highway on Fort Worth's North Side. This was his childhood playground. "Some of my best friends are buried here," he laments, stepping slowly over the lumpy green earth. A German shepherd stands guard over a tombstone, his former master. Bobby says they used to hang outlaws right here at the old hanging tree, before burying them. They'd have the trial right across the river at the courthouse.

Oakwood Cemetery provides Bobby's favorite birds'-eye view into downtown Fort Worth, across the Trinity River. Tall smokestacks rise up behind the train tracks, where "three niggers fell when they were building 'em... and my best friend is buried right there. He was shot between the eyes over a woman, back in the '50s.

"I still have some pretty good fights back at my motel, mostly with women," Bobby admits. The Rockwood stands behind Massey's, and is in considerably worse condition. The rooms run $12.95 per night, and each is equipped with an open space for a 1930s auto. "I do my best to keep a clean motel, but you can't always tell if they're prostitutes till they show their colors.

"Most of 'em white women, fight ya like a dog. I never hit a woman with my fist in my whole life. But I had one that sicced her damn dog on me. We had a knock-down, drag-out fight, she hung her fangs in my arm, almost bit it off—the woman, not the dog. Couldn't pry her jaws off. Boy, I mean I hit her back. She hadda let go to cuss me. And when she did, we rassled outta my office into the drive, and I'll be darned if she didn't sic that dog on me again. Little old poodle. I drug her to the front gate and tossed her out on Jacksboro Highway.

"Well, her blouse got tore off, she didn't have a bra on, but there wasn't anything to see, believe me, flat chest. That tickled me. I laughed and said, 'Lookit there!' She had two tattoos above where's supposed to be some female stuff, that said, '*Have Fun.*'

"'I'll tell you one thing, you Jacksboro Highway ho',' I told her, 'you better git down the highway, or next time I'm gonna fight you like a man.'"

The old-timers left on the Jax are so folksy, it's hard to imagine they were reared in such violent times. "Coldest Beer and Friendliest People in Texas," reads the logo outside Massey's 21 Club. But the last of the mom-and-pop joints along Jacksboro—as well as the rest of America—will soon be homogenized into assembly-line malls. All of what is ethnic, regional or historic will disappear in the ongoing corporate Texas chainsaw massacre, dictated by demographic surveys, not human spirit. Fort Worth presents its yearly Pioneer Days in the stockyards, but it is for tourists. The unbroken thread of the real wild West will remain on Jacksboro Highway for about a year.

"Our time's runnin' out," laments Bobby Sitton, hunched over his beloved Massey's bar. "That highway's gonna git us." The state will pay them a "fair market price" for the land and building. "But we're not getting a damn thing for the loss of customers we built up for 50 years. They're even taking the Rockwood Christian Church across the street. Used to be the old Massey home place. We sold it to the church with an understanding they'd never start a crusade against us. Now, it looks like they gonna go down the chute, too, with us."

—*1989*

CHAPTER FOURTEEN

WINEDALE NATION

n 1992, when I began performing Monday nights at the Winedale Tavern on Lower Greenville Avenue, it was Skid Row's royal palace in Dallas. There, some patrons behave as if just released from Parkland Hospital's observation ward; others, as though sprung from the dog pound. The audience is the show, and favorite evenings are those in which gorgeous, albeit demented, young girls sit interspersed with babbling, nose-bleeding derelicts. No matter where I'm booked, I try not to miss this engagement.

Playing for the homeless seemed a noble cause when I filled in one night for local songwriter-emcee Bob Ackerman. I agreed to cover one more Monday—but have extended my run three years.

Opened in 1985 by local restaurateur, Lota Dunham, the Winedale was conceived as a red-tablecloth "class" establishment. Indeed, it initially drew the Dallas Opera, being close to Nero's, the opera company's favorite Italian restaurant. But as the Dallas Opera began its slow decline in the late '80s, the Winedale began to attract a more derelict element. One can imagine Lota's trepidation, her dreams of polite society sipping Pouilly Fuisse giving way to a posse of dust-bowl panhandlers and Reagan-era homeless, who celebrate the art of alcoholism. Gone were the tablecloths. The Winedale became the Last Stop for those banned from every other bar on Greenville Avenue. The only beer joint on Greenville open at 7 a.m. No poor bastard became truly homeless until he was banned from the Winedale.

The quintessential Winedale man of this era was Lance. Though homeless, he had a debonair gait, like a movie pirate. In fact, he had one eye. When on the rebound, he carried himself with dignity, wore an eyepatch, bathed, slicked back his hair. Although he slept outdoors behind dumpsters, he managed to assemble a natty outfit. In this mode, Lance could actually score a slow dance with one of the Winedale's *femmes fatales*.

But just as often, he was on a downslide, lost his eyepatch and exposed an empty black socket, a grim abyss within his head. There was a shrivelled mess of skin around this black hole. Without the eyepatch, this cockeyed look was downright menacing to women he stared down. The socket had a hypnotic effect, and women found themselves staring back helplessly, before turning away in revulsion.

A hard-looking 42, Lance estimated he'd been in jail 250 times. These included overnight drunk tanks, three-day weekends, 10-day psychiatric observations. His longest stretch was three years at Rahway, New Jersey. "Do your time in a county jail," he advised, "stay away from the Federal pen."

A Monday or two might pass without Lance. Then he'd proudly saunter in, freshly sprung from Lew Sterrett Justice Center.

"You don't seem like a bad guy, Lance," I'd say. "What could possibly have put you there this time?"

"Tickets," was his stock answer.

It was known that Lance held a job in construction during his youth, and that he was good. Building contractors, impressed with his suave demeanor, offered construction work. Lance graciously accepted jobs, toasting a beer to salvation. But he never showed up. He was determined to live off the streets, banishing the work ethic forever.

"I'm sitting here because I ain't all there," he would often say at the bar, pointing to his brain.

Early on during my tenure at this deceptively humble shotgun bar, I noticed Winedale bartenders burn out fast. In my first six months, four were committed to convalescence or rehab clinics. I regretted losing barkeep Tim Nelson, a scrappy little red-bearded fellow.

"A round of waters for the house, on me!" I'd announce, through the PA, after the crowd had drummed along on the bar counter, to my acoustic take on"Wipeout."

"We're outta water," Tim would bellow. "But the first drink's on God." Free beers were served to Jezebels twice his size. He struck out with all of them.

At first, Tim ascribed to good bartending theory: if you miss a customer trying to order his first beer or two, you lose him for the night. Once he's had two, he'll likely stay for four or five. But this strategy was abandoned while Tim disappeared to the bar next door, downing more shots each week. (The Winedale has no hard liquor license.) Long before last call, he slumbered on the silver beer refrig, curled up in fetal position, hands angelically tucked under his head. Rouse him awake to order a Coke, he'd glare at you like you were insane. He eventually left the asylum to the inmates, letting gutter alcoholics fetch their own beers on the honor system.

The day after Tim was mugged while wandering disoriented up Maple Avenue, his friends arranged an "intervention," committing him to the V.A. rehab hospital. He stuck with the program, and began to excel at landscaping chores.

Screamin' Sadie, my second Monday night bartender, feared no man. She described half of her job as being "a professional escort to the door" for the unruly. Sadie 86'ed an average of five guys per Monday night, swiftly and without incident. She was a strict elementary schoolmarm presiding over older men with arrested developments.

But the customer who caused her the most turmoil was an elegant bejewelled Highland Park matron who always came undone during my acoustic rendition of "Tequila." She danced the length of the bar, Egyptian Pee Wee-style, fishing out her tits. Winos went bonkers, more showing up each week. But our gal Sadie felt inclined to uphold some specific TABC license required when both beer and boobs are served. Citing bureaucratic regulations, Sadie evicted her each week, soon as the tits debuted.

Next week, the Highland Park woman's Jaguar rolled up to the Winedale curb. The mystery dame never fraternized with our old hippies or wino regulars. Aloof and silent, she awaited her cue—the opening chords of "Tequila," originally played by Glen Campbell in the Champs.

By the fourth week of her midlife crisis, "Tequila" became my most popular request. "Go, baby, go!" clapped the winos. The lady stripped starkers this time, before Sadie could banish her for good ("We could lose our license," Sadie explained). To the groaning regret of many a derelict, bulky pop art collages were later suspended low from the bar ceiling. They prevent countertop Slut Dancing to this day.

The pressures took a fast toll on Sadie, who began to escort regulars out the door for imagined infractions. After six weeks, she cracked worse than Tim. Tanking up on shots next door, she returned plastered, crawling along the bar, her own breasts dangling out of her blouse, screaming "Fuck you!" to anyone who dared order a drink. She was promptly relieved, the management graciously arranging a long stay in a rest home. She was last reported doing fine, excelling in arts and crafts.

My third barkeep, an Irishman who came to America to work, was gung-ho to replace Sadie. He was a personable, cheerful rugby player in top shape. He cracked within a month, and booked passage to Asia Minor, which he planned to cross on foot.

Next came Pedro, a hardened, humorless pro who worked other shifts at the Winedale. His sideline business was stenciling house addresses on sidewalks. "Everybody needs their address painted, but don't do it themselves," he said, boasting that he'd cornered the market. He came to work in freshly pressed Arrow shirts, with a trim goatee and splash of witch hazel. An Aramis man.

Pedro prided himself on his utter refusal to ever "take shit from anybody." Yet Pedro adopted a generous "three strikes" rule of crowd control. Some bum got two chances. He might whisper sweet nothings in some mortified lady's ear. He might jump on stage, or emit some hair-raising yelp. Hyperactive dancers who looked like they might screw themselves into the floor got a strike. Whatever, Pedro issued an order to stop. By the third violation, Pedro threw his thumb up for strike three and hollered, "You're outta here!" He'd scale his side of the bar, arguing chest to chest with a grizzled old offender. "And I don't take no lip!" came Pedro, finger-poking his man out the door. Last words were always reserved for the perennial wino's threat, "I'll be back!"

For a while, it was argued as to whether the Winedale should become a "one-strike" place—because once troublemakers demonstrate they're willing to take strike two, they're on a roll. As musical chair, I felt obliged to remain uninvolved—other than playing "Howdy Doody Time" during bouncings. It was honor enough having a guy like Lance in the audience who'd spend his last few bucks nursing a couple of beers to hear me play some blues. This meant sacrificing a $4 room at the men's shelter and sleeping under the I-30 bridge. A quarter flipped into my tip jar from a homeless gent touched me more than a crisp hundred from a doctor or rich redneck.

The Winedale sisterhood included young regulars Nellie and Tara, who were fairly skilled at glomming drinks. They never paid or tipped. They smiled upon impoverished men as long as it took to fish out their beggar's change and order the girls beers. Then they abandoned the suckers for the pool table.

Nellie, a top-heavy *brunehilde*, was the daughter of a once-renowned Dallas bar owner—a testament as to why children shouldn't be raised in bars. By the end of the night, she'd slink out with a different vagrant, her eyes cast down in vacant disgrace. Next week she'd return with a black eye, bruises or stitches on her head. As soon as one black eye healed, she had an uncanny penchant for acquiring another.

"Fell off my bicycle," was her stock answer.

Tara, her bosom buddy, hadn't a clue that she was indeed attractive. With a low self-image and slumped shoulders, she turned haughty and sarcastic toward males. Nellie and Tara performed an ongoing routine for my benefit, a mock invitation to their hot tub back at the house. But they were often evicted as nuisance tenants, moving from apartment to apartment like two alley cats with suitcases.

Tara and Nellie often took barstools adjacent to the plywood stage, dreamily pencil-sketching themselves naked by their imaginary hot tub. Blushing, they dropped deranged pickup lines in my tip jar ("Hey, baby, I'd like to eat the peanuts outta your shit."). Tara deposited sketches of genitalia into my jar. I tried to persuade them to stalk Reverend Horton Heat instead of me.

Whenever I announced a Ladies Choice "Dance With Lance," it was Tara who obliged him. The Winedale's top drink scammer, 21 years old, blushing on Lance's shoulder, misfits at the high school prom they never attended. Lance's song was "Sleepwalk," a slow, crotch-grinding chestnut I played in Greenwich Village with doo-wop group City Limits. (Back then, our diesel-dyke impresario of several lesbian cabarets softly professed, "I kissed my first goil to that song in high school.")

Follow-up Winedale dance announcements included a Necrophiliac's Choice, as well as singalong sections isolating just the ladies, then just the men, then the ex-cons, those out on parole, those with one eye or leg, etc. This was no joke. The Winedale resembled the Howdy Doody Peanut Gallery, shot to hell.

Pedro never cracked a smile at my smart-ass routines. Though he'd outlasted my previous three bartenders, I noticed his patience thinning. He was Born to Bounce, especially older, enfeebled violators who came for the music, not the beer. Order a water and he would begin the umpire shtick. Ultimatums came quicker. He communed with a few scowling cab drivers at the back of the bar, relating how he bounced out truckers and bikers twice his size, at previous bar jobs. The cabbies responded with tales of customer altercations that led to fist fights and macings. Pedro's corner turf became a separate Winedale nation from my acid vaudeville show up front.

"Lance could make something of himself," Pedro often complained, "but he don't want to work." If Lance arrived without the eyepatch, Pedro disapproved. He considered this uncouth grooming, improper etiquette during his shift. He reminded people that he ran this bar, and how all the street people knew not to mess with Pedro. But he usually kept his distance from Lance. "That guy can take care of himself. I wouldn't want to mess with him."

The Winedale is a shabby oasis, detached from the club circuit. I prefer its sublime natural acoustics to most rock clubs. If a stranger interrupts my set making unrealistic demands ("Play some Smothers Brothers, goddamnit!"), a protective layer of hobos will form to my defense.

"Play your own shit!" cry my alcoholic defenders, deflecting James Taylor requests from SMU students. My three ultimate taboos: James Taylor, Cat Stevens and Jim Croce. This unholy trinity comprises the musically illiterate's microscopic vision of what someone with an acoustic guitar is supposed to cover.

I always felt secure that if I ever ended up overnight at Lew Sterrett, some guardian hobo from the Winedale would surely be there. Most likely Lance, who saw jail as a paid vacation from the streets. He awoke behind a dumpster most mornings, happy as a lark, amazed to open his eyes and hear the chirping of birds.

"Always thankful no one waltzed by with a crowbar to bash my head in," he told me. He ripped tubes from his body when he awoke in hospitals, propositioned nurses and chuckled his way down the back stairs with stolen drugs—anxious to make Monday at the Winedale.

Lance claimed to have shared a cell in California with David Crosby. If his drug and legal problems weren't enough, Crosby must have been bombarded by Lance's song lyrics. He pulled crumpled sheets of paper from his trousers, rattling off fresh verses composed in jail, full of real-life hardship and hobo angst. He'd break into a thumb-popping hard sell, slinging lyrics at me while I was onstage, in the middle of a guitar solo or between songs. Since Crosby, Stills, Nash & Lance never materialized, he hoped to join forces with me.

A few homeless regulars, disenfranchised though they were, felt compelled to go to bat for my career. One old leprechaun, reminiscent of Walter Huston in *Treasure of Sierra Madre*, showed up with a million-dollar record deal in the works. He enlisted backing from McDonald's, whom he alleged had finally taken a shine to my anti-jingle, "Thanksgiving At McDonald's In Times Square." The McDonald's leprechaun claimed to be tight, in his pre-wino days, with McDonald's founder Ray Kroc. Every week he returned with progress reports and recording studio dates. Then someone recognized the wino from his days handing out discount Chicken McNuggets coupons in the West End. His sphere of influence ended there.

Called on the delusion, he cackled so hard, I thought he'd need a straitjacket. Lance, who himself had some TV deal in the works for me, wasn't charmed, and punched the poor guy out, which sent him scurrying off from the Winedale forever.

Pedro's nerves disintegrated slowly but steadily, like shock absorbers on a New York taxi. One night a young girl got onstage to sing "Roadhouse Blues." It was her first time onstage; she dreamt of being a folk singer. Some little stone freak hippie in front became overly taken with her. "She's great!" he exploded, continuing to applaud after everyone else finished. "She's great… and I suck! She's great, and we all suck! This place sucks. You suck, I suck, and fuck us all!"

At surreal moments of truth like this, when someone was about to go over the edge, the whole bar would come to a hush. Pedro took charge, hands upon hips, not about to take shit. "All right, pipe down." (Strike one.)

"She's great!" came the little freak, stalking toward Pedro. "You suck!" he ranted in some meth-driven rage. "You suck, she's great, she's better than all of us!" he went on, now jabbing his finger.

"You're outta here!" came Pedro, hopping over the bar.

"I suck!" the freak shot back, continuing his odd outburst with passive aggression. The guy insulted himself profusely, which confused Pedro enough that he shrugged and headed back behind the bar.

Lance was inevitably banned from the Winedale. Though he behaved commendably on my night, he apparently crossed over the line, prompting another evening's bartender to brand him persona non grata. If one Winedale bartender saw fit to ban a customer, all other bartenders upheld the decision. Lance, sans patch, may have whispered one of his hair-raising sweet nothings into women's ears at the bar. ("*How 'bout lettin' Lance in yer pants? Any chance?*")

Thereafter, Lance began to appear like an apparition at the door each Monday night, peering in like a pauper at a Christmas store. "Hang in there, Lance," I'd announce through the mike. "This ain't no Shangri-La, this ain't no promised land. It's just the Winedale." A round of "amen's" rumbled from the privileged class inside. But a tear fell down Lance's cheek from his one good eye. Cold, weather-beaten, having lost weight, he was too cowed to enter. My wife, who considers Monday a school night, had come on a rare visit. He gingerly tipped the front door and whispered to her, "Is it okay if I open it a little, to just listen?"

With Pedro's threshold for tomfoolery down to one strike, more regulars received permanent evictions. Especially non-drinking music fans, stripped of citizenship at the Last Stop on Greenville Avenue. Winedale Country was off-limits. Banishment from the London Tavern, Service Bar, Nero's or Simply Fondue was taken in stride. But Winedale banishment was a humiliation most found hard to accept. Excommunicated winos and old hippies paced before the window each Monday, pining to come in, awaiting forgiveness, shouting their favorite requests from outside.

I spoke up for Lance, but Pedro wouldn't budge. Ironically, it was another bartender who banished Lance, and neither Lance nor Pedro had a clue as to why.

"Speak to Pete," Pedro shouted to Lance outside, "clear it up with him. Until he says yes, you can't enter."

"What'd I do?" Lance would ask week after week, from the door. He claimed not to know the bartender who banned him, couldn't fathom the infraction. But Pedro held steadfast.

I played "Thanksgiving At McDonald's" each week for Lance, who beamed at the door with other undesirables, slapping each other five. Among my sidewalk audience was Ray the Poetry Mugger. A Black street hustler, he cornered yuppies on Greenville Avenue with his tip jar, jabbering psycho poetry as they stared vacantly. Stalking college coffeehouses, he'd hold a whole table hostage with an epic like "The Days Of Your Week": "*Monday is a work day, berserk day, get up early wash yo' shirt day...*"

I often bring traveling guest musicians to the Winedale. A recovering Texas blues guitarist made the pilgrimage. "Give this man a hand," I told the audience, as he strapped on his guitar. But he'd fallen off the wagon that night, and fell, mid-song, off the stage. He collapsed in sections, out cold from a combination of beer and hard dope.

"Is that the blues?" asked two ingenuous SMU boys, hovering over his body, seeking musical knowledge.

"Not exactly," I said. "B.B. King don't collapse onstage. Now, give this man a hand."

Pedro began giving me the brush-off. Whenever I ordered a drink he'd say, "Get it yourself." When I finally got my own beer, he saw this as the ultimate affront to his authority. A three-strike offense. The worst infraction a musician can commit against a club is to help himself to a beer. Might throw off the books. He rallied his corner of the bar against me. A Mexican who ran illicit cockfights began flipping cryptic hand signals my way. I knew one of us—me or Pedro—had to go.

Then Lance appeared at the door. It was winter, and he'd bottomed out with the shakes. He stared into the bar mournfully. I was whipping out final songs of the night, before two dozen hardcore customers. Suddenly, Lance began a game of cat and mouse. He opened the door. Pedro put his hands on hips. Then Lance took one step over the border line of public sidewalk into the establishment. Pedro shot out his thumb: "*Outta here!*"

At this moment, the crowd started rooting for Lance. I began my oft-played bouncer's march—"Howdy Doody Time" (sung to "Tra-La-La-Boom-De-Ay"). The whole bar, rather than hushing, became the Peanut Gallery, and I was Buffalo Bob Smith. The joint went bonkers, all the winos clapping and singing along. Especially Lance, a demonic, overjoyed grin on his face, stomping an Irish jig. He danced into the Winedale singing, "It's Howdy Doody time, it's Howdy Doody time!" Pedro, summoning reserve strength at the end of the night, bolted over the bar, locked an arm around Lance's elbow and backpedaled him out. A weakened, underweight Lance danced madly backward, belting out the chorus. He fell in the gutter.

Satisfied that he bounced the guy, Pedro regained his authority, brushed his hands of the affair. He took his position behind the bar. And who should come goose-stepping back in but Lance, more berserk with Howdy Doody than ever. The rafters shook with choruses of "Doody."

Another shoving match. But this time, with the entire Winedale Nation's energy against him, the bartender didn't win. Pedro's shoulders went limp, his resolve defeated. He backed down. He took shit. Lance was home free. It was truly Howdy Doody Time at the Winedale.

Something in Pedro died that night. He mumbled under his breath. He told me I was through playing the Winedale. But he was fired the next day.

After a month of soul-searching, he recovered somewhat and was rehired to work other shifts. Word has it he's been raising chickens. (And he won't take shit from poultry.)

My current bartender, Steve Vail, has been with me two years running. His stock warning to panhandlers: "This is not a soup kitchen for the alcoholically impaired."

The demographics have changed a bit over the last two years, shamefully upscaled. But even a poorly attended evening can take a sudden surreal twist.

Not long ago, a tour bus pulled up at midnight unloading 50 French gynecologists. They were impeccably dressed in smart designer outfits, in Dallas for a vaginal summit. How they happened upon the Winedale I'll never know, but they lustily reveled in their discovery of an authentic American dive.

I'd luckily brought my Silvertone and Danelectro guitars, drenching them with Texas blues. One doctor spotted the first 50 beers with a hundred dollar bill. The next 50 longnecks were popped open on credit. By 2 a.m., ties loosened, sweat circling beneath their pits, they'd danced and enjoyed life, *bon vivants* free from the constraints of the medical establishment. It was the only night I ever saw bartender Steve get looped.

When the last of the gynecologists had boarded the departing bus, tearfully waving *au revoir*, Steve realized they stiffed us on the beers. As is peculiar to

France with its frugal anti-tipping tradition, there wasn't one penny in my or the bartender's tip jars. Feeling diplomatic, I was glad they chose the Winedale for a taste of America over the plastic tourism of a Hard Rock Cafe.

Rarely does Steve have to bounce anyone, as he is beloved by all and doesn't need to assert much authority. Once I saw him take out his black midget bat when a sinewy mental patient refused to leave. Steve gave him his three strikes, but the guy wouldn't budge. He just presented his head, called Steve's bluff, awaiting the crack of the wood. When Steve wouldn't strike, he left disappointed. Steve already excels as a sailboat skipper.

Lance collapsed dead on Christmas in a construction foreman's car. It was the first day of a job he actually showed up for.

—1995

ALSO BY JOSH ALAN FRIEDMAN

BOOKS

Tales of Times Square
Any Similarity To Persons Living or Dead is Purely Coincidental
  (comics anthology, art by Drew Friedman)
Warts And All
  (comics anthology, art by Drew Friedman)
Now Dig This: The Unspeakable Writings of Terry Southern
  (anthology edited with Nile Southern)

ALBUMS

Famous & Poor
The Worst!
Blacks 'n' Jews
Josh Alan Band

NOW AVAILABLE FROM FERAL HOUSE!